Ayrton Senna's
PRINCIPLES OF RACE DRIVING

Ayrton Senna's PRINCIPLES OF RACE DRIVING

HAZLETON PUBLISHING

This English-language edition first published in 1993 by
Hazleton Publishing
Richmond Hill
Richmond
Surrey TW10 6RE

© Hazleton Securities Ltd 1993

First published in Italian by La Mille Miglia Editrice, Brescia, Italy

© 1991 Ayrton Senna da Silva Promotions Ltd
© 1991 La Mille Miglia Editrice

Printed in Hong Kong by Dai Nippon

Translated by Norman Howell

ISBN: 1-874557-40-3

DISTRIBUTORS

United Kingdom
Bookpoint Limited
39 Milton Park
Abingdon
Oxfordshire OX14 4TD

North America
Motorbooks International
PO Box 2
729 Prospect Avenue
Osceola
Wisconsin 54020, USA

South Africa
Motorbooks
341 Jan Smuts Avenue
Craighall Park
Johannesburg

Australia
Technical Book and Magazine Co. Pty
289-299 Swanston Street
Melbourne
Victoria 3000

Universal Motor Publications
c/o Automoto Motoring Bookshop
152-154 Clarence Street
Sydney 2000
New South Wales

New Zealand
David Bateman Limited
'Golden Heights'
32-34 View Road
Glenfield
Auckland 10

CONTENTS

	FOREWORD	6
CHAPTER 1	THE DRIVING POSITION	9
CHAPTER 2	CORNERING: THE RACING LINE	25
CHAPTER 3	CORNERING: CONTROLLING THE CAR	50
CHAPTER 4	BRAKING	55
CHAPTER 5	ACCELERATION AND GEARCHANGING	61
CHAPTER 6	MAKING THE BEST USE OF YOUR TYRES	69
CHAPTER 7	BEYOND THE LIMIT: ACCIDENTS	77
CHAPTER 8	DRIVING IN THE WET AND IN DIFFICULT CONDITIONS	85
CHAPTER 9	TESTING AND THE CAR'S DEVELOPMENT	95
CHAPTER 10	A DRIVER'S NATURAL TALENT: TO BE A GOOD TEST DRIVER	101
CHAPTER 11	HOW TO INTERPRET THE CAR'S BEHAVIOUR	107
CHAPTER 12	SETTING UP THE CAR	113
CHAPTER 13	THE CHOICE OF GEAR RATIOS	119
CHAPTER 14	THE WARM-UP	123
CHAPTER 15	THE LINE-UP AND FORMATION LAP	127
CHAPTER 16	THE START	131
CHAPTER 17	THE OPENING LAPS	147
CHAPTER 18	OVERTAKING	151
CHAPTER 19	USING THE SLIPSTREAM	163
CHAPTER 20	PIT SIGNALS AND RACE TACTICS	167
CHAPTER 21	FLAG SIGNALS	171
CHAPTER 22	FITNESS TRAINING	175
CHAPTER 23	DIET	189
CHAPTER 24	PSYCHOLOGY	199

Foreword

When I received the invitation to write this book, I immediately accepted the challenge, though I knew of the difficulties I would have in putting down on paper all I had learned in seven years of karting and almost 13 of motor racing. Writing has never been my forte. I prefer reading what other people write, especially when the subject is linked to my sport. But I thought that with the help of a specialist journalist I would manage to get the message across to all those who love driving at a more advanced level.

Another reason for my involvement in this project is the lack, in bookshops all over the world, of valid textbooks on the technique of driving on track. Books which could be of real help to beginners are rare indeed. Specialist journalists prefer to write about what goes on behind the scenes at the Grands Prix and about the drivers' personal lives.

As you will see, the publishers and myself have aimed for a technical book, with good illustrations, with the objective of giving good advice and guiding all those who are hoping to enter the world of motor racing.

In this book you will learn many of my racecraft secrets: how to overtake, how to drift and skid in a controlled manner on fast bends, how to concentrate at the start of a race, how to set up the suspension and save your tyres, what I do to win pole position, and how to get fit for racing.

But let's not waste any more time. After this brief introductory lap, here's the green light for you to start reading. You will experience for the first time the sensation of being in a Formula 1 car at 300 kilometres an hour. I hope you won't have any accidents before coming to the end of this book, my first literary Grand Prix.

CHAPTER 1

THE DRIVING POSITION

A good driving position is essential in order to be able to express yourself and take advantage of the potential of a Formula 1 car. It's true that the cockpit space within a single-seater is a compromise that the driver has to accept, but if he has the opportunity he must try and have it custom made. This will enable him, at least in theory, to start with an advantage over his opponents.

A driver who is uncomfortable, who might have to drive with his legs held at an angle or too tucked in, will soon feel the heat and exhaustion and suffer, not because he has not prepared himself physically, but rather because he has overtired his limbs by making them work in unnatural positions.

Designers always have their good reasons for making the cockpits ever smaller: better aerodynamic efficiency, better torsional rigidity, these are important goals. If you are a young driver, it will be harder to make your thoughts heard. But in the quest for the optimum driving position, there are rules that are often disregarded by aspiring drivers.

The first of these is that none of the movements involving arms and legs should end with the limbs being fully stretched. These limbs should be naturally extended, neither fully stretched nor tucked in too much: this will enable them to apply their maximum strength. For example, when the left leg is on the clutch, at the end of the pedal's travel – which is in any case very short – it should not be fully extended; just as the right leg must not be hindered at knee height when the foot shifts from the throttle to the brake, or when executing a heel-and-toe manoeuvre.

The same goes for the arms, which must be allowed to exploit their potential fully. This is because, though a Formula 1 steering wheel cannot be compared to a road car, nevertheless in a Grand Prix one often reaches the 300

The position of the hands on the steering wheel is one of the first rudiments that a single-seater driver must learn at the beginning of his career. There are rules which indicate the correct position, but every driver will discover for himself the arrangement that allows him to exert pressure on the steering wheel in the most efficient way. A fundamental principle of driving is that the outside hand (shown in red) is the one which applies the most pressure when entering a bend, while the inside hand merely follows the movement. On exiting the bend, it is the inside hand which guides the movement to straighten the steering wheel. The illustration above shows diagramatically the sequence for a right-handed bend, while the one below is for a left-handed bend.

This is the correct hand position on the steering wheel of a Formula 1 car. The arms are not fully extended, but slightly bent. The grip is relaxed, the thumbs rest on the upper spokes, thus increasing the grip on the wheel. In this way the driver can retain perfect control of the car. This position is commonly known as 'a quarter past nine'.

The hand position during a gearchange. The left hand, which has to keep the car in a straight line, stays on the steering wheel. The right hand changes gears. The photograph shows clearly how the right arm, though extended, is not rigidly at full stretch. The arms are slightly bent, allowing the driver to absorb the strain of driving more easily and to perform flowing movements.

Ayrton Senna demonstrates the movements a driver has to make for a tight left-hand bend. The outside hand exerts pressure on the steering wheel, while the left hand follows through. The lock, always very direct on a Formula 1 car, allows the driver to indulge in a 'forbidden' technique, at least in everyday driving: crossing the arms.

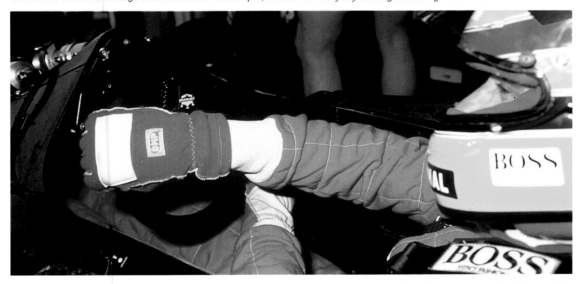

And here is the famous 'crossed arms' technique: the right arm (this is a left-hand bend) crosses over the left one. It's quite clear that this is a marginal position, which does not allow any more movement in steering the car through the bend, but it must be pointed out that the extremely direct lock of a Formula 1 car allows a tight bend, even a hairpin, to be taken using just this movement.

kilometres per hour mark.

Thus the arms, in the 'quarter past nine' position, the one used for the straights, must not be fully extended, but rather slightly bent. The distance between the torso and the steering wheel must be such that the elbow will touch the seat only when the arm has applied full lock in the execution of a turning manoeuvre. If the elbow is not able to reach such a position, or if it gets slightly stuck, it means the distance between the torso and steering wheel is less than ideal: in other words one is still too near the steering wheel.

In order to achieve the best driving position, it is essential to have a seat made which then becomes the ideal link between the driver and the cockpit. The quest for the best driving position and the best seat is one to which you must devote a lot of time. It is very tiring to lower yourself into the cockpit time after time for hours on end, but it is essential. With today's technology it is possible to mould a seat to the driver's body which, together with the footrest and the six-point harness, will enable the driver and car to be one entity; it will also allow the driver to feel the slightest irregularity of the track and every single reaction of the car.

Only in this way will the driver have a direct and honest relationship with the car, and be able to extend his instinct and feelings to the four tyres touching the ground.

The footrest is an essential accessory for a racing car. It must be at the same level as the clutch pedal, to enable the foot to shift with only one movement towards the right, onto the clutch, thus saving the time involved in bringing the foot from a lower level to that of the pedal. Once the foot has pressed and depressed the clutch, it must always return to the footrest – or, in these days of semi-automatic gearboxes, should always stay there.

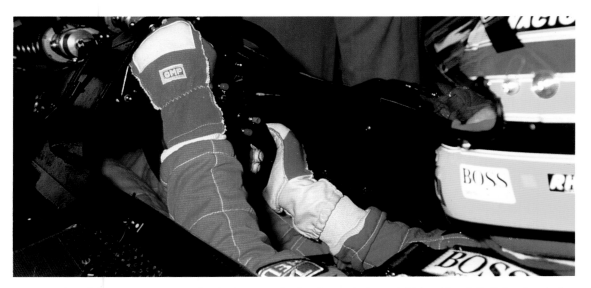

Here we picture the same movement, but in the opposite direction, entering a right-hand bend. Both hands grip the steering wheel, the thumbs are resting on the spokes. The movement is started without moving the hands from the rim. Here again it is the outside arm which leads the steering wheel, while the other simply follows through.

The 'crossed arms' technique has just been used in a right-hand bend: the left hand grips the wheel, while the right, as seen in the photo, is open and does not hinder the movement. The thumbs are still resting on the spokes. This way the movement is relaxed and the bottom hand, as soon as the upper one moves back, is ready to push as well and bring the steering wheel back to its original position.

This is how the pedals are arranged in the tight space of a Formula 1 cockpit: the throttle, clutch, brake and footrest. In this confined area the feet must move with great speed. Here we are on a straight, with the right foot, the one on the left in the photo, pushing the throttle. The other stays firmly placed on the footrest.

Here we start to brake: the foot presses firmly on the brake pedal, having left the throttle – the movement is shown by the white arrow. The other foot is still on the footrest and has not yet moved onto the clutch. We are still at the initial phase, before the gearchange, which comes before entering the corner and will start in a fraction of a second.

We are still braking. The right foot presses the brake pedal, but at the same time has rotated towards the outside, and with the side of the sole, presses the throttle; meanwhile the left foot has moved to the clutch to change into a lower gear. This manoeuvre is known as 'heel and toe', even though as we've seen it should be called 'sole/sole'.

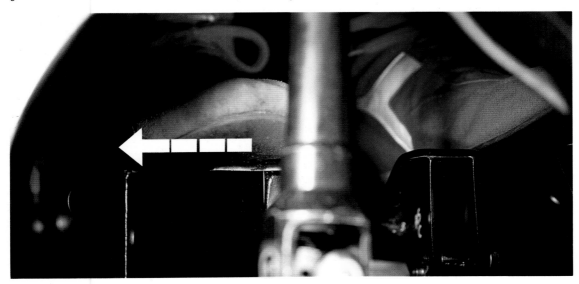

The gear is in, the left foot (on the right-hand side of the picture) goes back to the footrest, while the right foot leaves the brake pedal to return to the throttle. This picture may give the impression of a very slow movement, but in fact this is done, many times and in quick succession, in thousandths of a second, especially on twisty circuits like Monaco.

The footrest has another function: to make the driver more comfortable inside the cockpit, especially when taking a fast bend. Not every Formula 1 car has one, mainly for space reasons, and this is without doubt a fault.

The last topic of this chapter is the position of the hands on the steering wheel. To this end, an old rule still applies: when on a straight, the hands should be held in the 'quarter past nine' position; in other words you should imagine the steering wheel as a clock and look for 9.15, which on the steering wheel in a racing car corresponds to the two highest spokes.

On Formula 1 cars the steering is always very direct, so that the hands are only very rarely moved from that position, usually just to change gear. And of course with semi-automatic gearboxes they are not moved at all. In the case of the hairpin bend at Loews in Monte Carlo, the old rule of never crossing the arms would require a hand to be moved, to let it slide and then immediately grip again, as the other hand loosens the grip and slides back to the 9.15 position, the one which allows the best degree of control. But this would be a great waste of time, and it is necessary only on road-going cars, which have a less direct lock. A swift cross-over is a better technique, and with practice it loses all its perceived danger.

In tackling a bend, say a right-hand one, pressure is applied on the steering wheel with the left hand, while the right just follows through: on the exit of the bend, it will be the

What you see here is an indispensible part of finding the correct driving position: Ayrton Senna trying out a seat in a Formula 1 car, in this instance a McLaren. In order to find the right position, it is necessary to endure a long and tiring process. But once you have found it, you are able to 'feel' the car's reactions with the seat of your pants.

Senna

BOSS
MEN'S FASHION

Ma.

right hand which will be putting pressure to straighten the steering wheel. So as a general rule we may say that it is the outside hand which leads the car into the bend, while the inside one leads it out.

Leaving aside the rule for a moment, it is necessary to highlight the importance of the speed of execution. Thus instead of an orthodox hand position which slows down movements, it is preferable to adopt another position, one which will make the driver more comfortable. Only in this way will he attain the necessary speed and maintain whatever natural ability to improvise he may possess.

Pages 20-21: *This picture highlights all that has been written in this chapter about the driving position. The movement is fluid and develops smoothly, without any effort because the arms are neither tucked in nor overly extended. If these rules are observed, it is possible to drive the length of a Grand Prix, around 300 kilometres, without tiring either the arms or the legs too much.*

In this picture, taken from above, the narrowness of a modern Formula 1 car, in this case a McLaren MP4/6-Honda, is quite obvious. The cockpit fairing extends to cover the arms and shoulders of the driver. From this angle it is also possible to see how the hands rest on the steering wheel and the arms are not over-extended.

CHAPTER 2

CORNERING: THE RACING LINE

The racing tracks on which F1 cars do battle are by definition a series of bends interrupted by straights of varying length. Given that the idea is to lap in the least amount of time, the way you take corners becomes fundamental, not least because the first thing to understand is that an error on a bend is always paid for in lost hundredths of a second.

The racing line is the imaginary line which marks the path of the car. The straighter it is, in other words the wider the radius, the more the difference between the speed of the car before the bend and after the bend will be reduced. Thus it is essential to find the ideal racing line, or trajectory, for each bend. There is only one and it allows us to round off the angle of a corner. As an example, let's look at a 90-degree bend. Instead of taking it by following its direction exactly, it is possible to cut it and take a wider radius: in this way we will exit at higher speed. By doing this we have also encountered another fundamental principle of circuit driving: you have to use the full breadth of the track. And beyond too, as in the case of hairpins and especially chicanes. To cut a bend means looking for a racing line which corresponds to a corner with a wider radius than the one we are driving through. The car will then find new points of reference.

There are three fundamental points in a bend: the turning-in point, or start of the corner, which can be described as the end of the straight; the apex, where the car brushes past the kerb on the inside of the corner, the slowest part of the bend; and the exit, or end of the corner, when the car begins to travel in a straight line again, or when the bend can be said to have finished and another started. In this case, the exit (the fastest part of a corner) and the entry point of the next bend obviously

This picture shows the car at the apex of the corner; a few inches later the inside front wheel, lighter than the outside load-bearing one, will climb slightly over the kerb. This line has been chosen to straighten the bend as much as possible and thus allow it to be taken as fast as possible. Sometimes, because of the traffic on the track, it is hard to take the ideal racing line.

overlap.

To sum up, we could say that a bend is always taken by going first to the outside, then to the inside, then to the outside again, using as much of the track as possible and maybe even climbing up on the kerb. It's true that in modern Grand Prix racing the kerbs are best avoided. We have reached the point where the flat-bottomed cars are almost caressing the road surface in the search for ever-more ground effect. The sparks which they leave in their wake are seen more clearly and more frequently than a few years ago. Today we maintain contact with the ground not only with the tyres but also with the bottom of the car, and riding up on the kerb can lead to the possibility of mechanical damage, which is rarely worth risking.

The ideal line in a 90-degree corner is in theory the curve with the maximum constant radius, which links the three main points of the bend with the same curving radius.

Within this racing line we have to get used to identifying the three phases already mentioned which correspond to the three main points. This is a very important distinction, which enables us to embark on a deeper analysis of the car and the way we drive. This is how we will identify any defects and subsequently put them right.

The maximum constant radius around a bend is not always the most effective solution. It is certainly useful when approaching a big fast bend, when there isn't much acceleration at the exit. But when the bend is slow or medium-fast, and especially if it is followed by a long straight, the line must be changed to allow you to accelerate earlier. In this case the apex will not correspond to the geometric apex (which divides the inside of the bend into two equal parts in accordance with the line which bisects the angle of the bend), but

In this picture the rear wheel is at the apex of the bend, while the front wheel has just passed it. This is when acceleration begins. The photo was taken in Belgium, at Spa-Francorchamps, a fast and difficult circuit which also features some slow bends, like this one called La Source.

will be somewhat before it. Thus the cornering phase is brought forward by comparison with the maximum constant radius line and you can accelerate earlier.

Braking will have to be later, the entry phase will have a smaller radius and the exit phase – accelerating throughout – will have a variable radius line and will be longer than the equivalent phase in the case of the maximum constant radius line. This type of racing line is easier to understand if applied to a hairpin. which is where the most advantage is to be found: the time lost in the first and second phases is much less than the advantage given by accelerating earlier (giving rise to the old cliché 'to exit fast you have to enter slow'). The real apex varies in relation to the geometric apex depending on the tightness of

the bend. At a hairpin it will be brought forward by about 10 per cent of the length of the inside kerb; at a longer bend by up to 20 or 25 per cent.

In the case of a series of bends not interrupted by straights (the most obvious example is a chicane, but it could also be two bends close to each other or dependent on one another) the rules described so far are perfectly valid, but we need to introduce a new principle: the last bend always takes priority. In these cases you have to sacrifice the first bend in favour of the second (or of the last if there are more than two) because, as we have already seen, gain or loss are linked to the exit from the bend (or bends) and to the length of the following straight. For example, in the case of a chicane followed by a long straight (such as the first chicane at Monza) it will be necessary to sacrifice the exit of the

30

first section in order to be in a better position for the entry of the second and last part of the bend. In this way we will lose something at the start (where it is almost impossible to overtake anyway) so as to exit the second half with greater speed. And in the end, this is what matters.

In the reverse situation, when we have a long straight preceding two or more bends, we cannot sacrifice the first bend in order to favour those that follow because, due to the high speeds involved, the loss of time would be too great. Thus you have to brake as late as possible and take the maximum constant radius line in the first bend, knowing that the loss of time you will incur at the end of the straight following the bends (which we assume to be short) will be less than the advantage earned by taking the first bend as fast as possible.

One of the classic hairpin bends in Formula 1. This is Monte Carlo in front of the Loews Hotel. 1) Ayrton Senna sets up the bend after the straight; 2) he aims for the apex by tightening his line towards the kerb, which he reaches in 3). In the next phase, the driver begins to accelerate exiting the curve, 4) and 5), which will happen more decisively on the brief straight which comes before the next bend.

This wonderful photo taken from above, at the Detroit street circuit, shows in an obvious and practical way how you cut a corner to reach the apex, which will be on the left-hand page. On the track, the more you straighten a bend, the faster you will be.

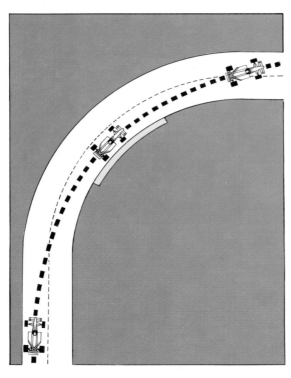

The difference in line between driving on the road and on the track is shown in this illustration. The driver at the wheel of a single-seater cuts the corner to achieve a higher travelling speed. The fainter line represents a normal line, which follows the radius of the bend, while the thicker line is the maximum constant radius, which allows for the maximum exit speed.

A single-seater driver must quickly get used to dividing a bend into three parts: the entry, the middle phase and the exit. In the illustrations below we have two examples of corners: on the left, the normal constant maximum radius bend; on the right the one which advances the middle phase. The latter permits the driver to bring forward the point of acceleration because the exiting phase is much straighter. Thus the car will already be faster when it reaches the straight.

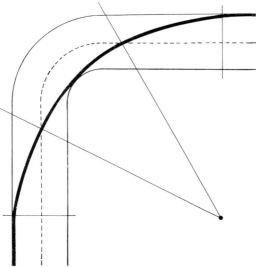

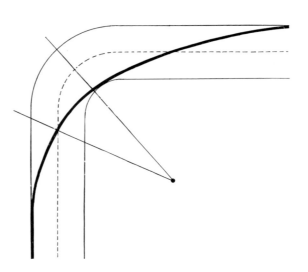

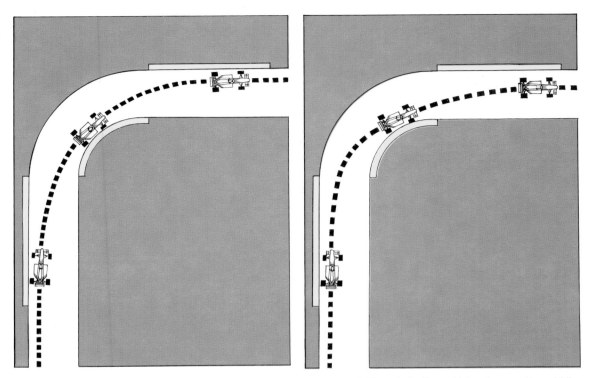

In these two illustrations you see the maximum constant radius line (left) and the line which advances the middle phase. The second is very useful, particularly for certain types of bend, such as medium-fast and slow corners and especially hairpins. For bends which do not require much acceleration at the exit, like wide sweeping bends which are taken flat out, the maximum constant radius line proves to be the most effective. When you bring forward the middle phase, you lose time because your line has a tighter radius, but in reality this loss is more than offset by your higher exit speed.

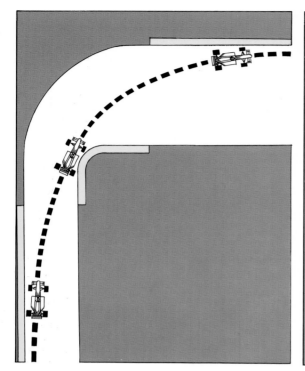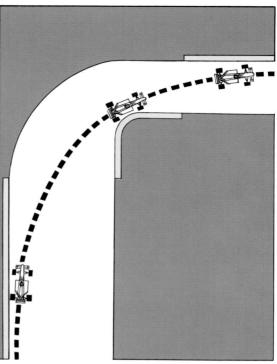

Years ago, when many of the tracks were sited at airfields and there were few permanent sites, it was common for drivers to come across bends like the one above, where the straight leading into the corner is narrower than the one after it. In this case the driver must take an early apex in order to exploit the full width of the track while exiting and thus gain speed.

This is the opposite case: the straight after the bend is narrower than the one before it. Here the driver must delay the entry to the corner so as not to run out of track at the exit. This situation will create a lower exit speed than that illustrated on the left. It is possible to compare this bend to one which has a tendency to tighten on exit, which is not uncommon on modern circuits.

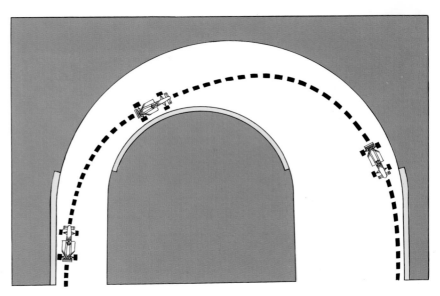

The illustration above shows a situation we find at modern Formula 1 tracks – for example the Parabolica at Monza, where the apex is taken early in comparison with the theoretical one, because the bend is linked to a straight which is much wider than the one leading into it. A similar line can be employed where it is possible to run wide at the exit.

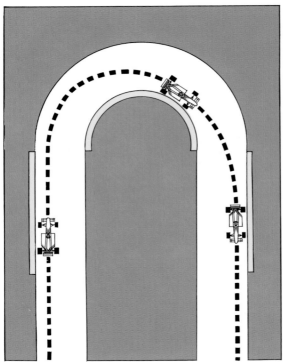

Left: The line with the early middle phase is often applied to a 90-degree bend. However, this kind of racing line is even more apt for a corner of the sort shown on the left. If you approach a hairpin bend where you need to accelerate strongly at the exit, it is important to start to turn in as early as possible: it is obvious that a car that is already pointing in the right direction, with the wheels at less of an angle, will be able to accelerate earlier.

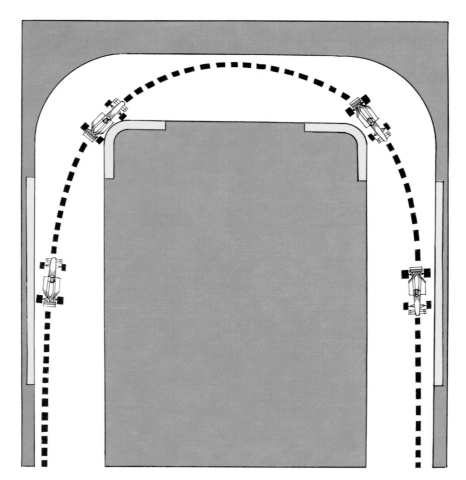

Something that happens quite often on race circuits is to find two bends linked by a short straight. So as not to lose speed, the driver must take both bends as if they were one. He will turn the steering wheel only once and will have only one racing line. Sometimes, in order to find the most fluid and natural line, a driver may choose not to exploit all of the track on the short straight, but stay instead in the middle. The illustration shows how the ideal racing line has to be set up.

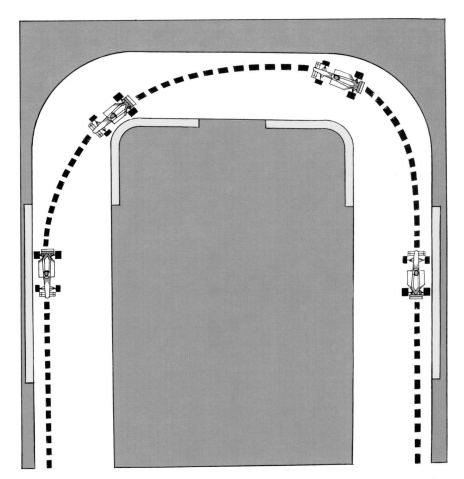

When two bends are linked by a short straight, it may not always be best to adopt the racing line described previously. It may be more effective to take the first bend away from the apex and instead aim for the apex of the next one. Here too the distance from the kerbs is dictated by a perfect line and exit. This technique is also useful when confronted with wide bends which tend to narrow near the end: by going to the kerb late we can maintain the car's speed and overcome the difficulties of a tightening bend.

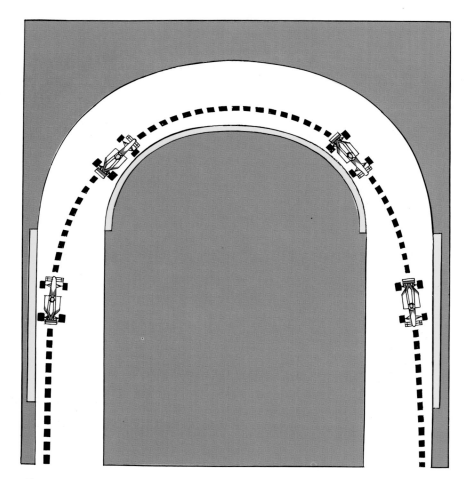

The accepted way to tackle a bend is for the car to brush the inside kerb once only and for the briefest of moments. Sometimes, though, it is necessary to stay on the inside, to follow the kerb for a great deal of its length, because the layout of the bend will not allow you to find the apex and then widen your line towards the outside. To execute this technique correctly a driver must turn into the corner early and move to the outside only when the bend is almost complete.

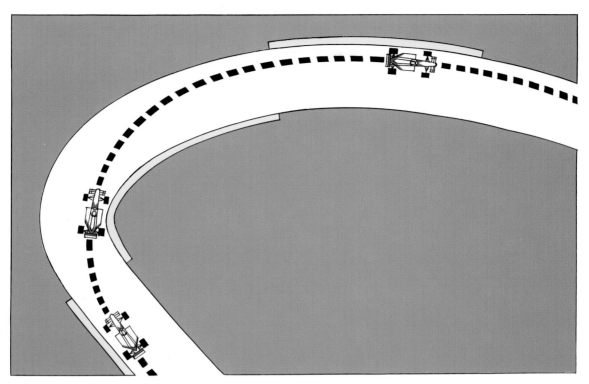

This is a variable radius bend, where the corner opens progressively after the apex. This is good for the driver because the bend opens just as the driver's own line does. In these cases you have to take an early apex and then concentrate on the natural line – which will have no reference points – in order to accelerate hard and progressively at the exit.

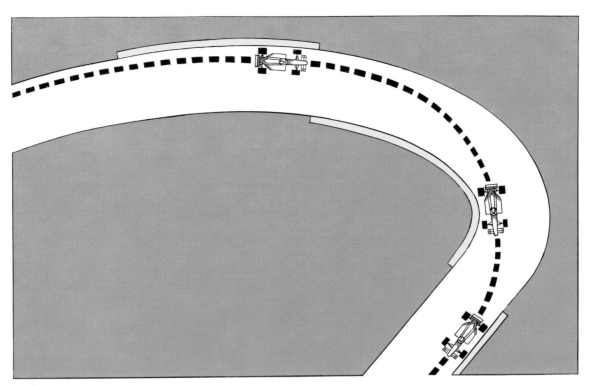

Variable radius curves aren't always an advantage for the driver, as is illustrated above. In this situation it is best to stay wide on entry and go to the apex relatively late. If there is a long straight before the bend, it will be possible to delay the point of entry and of braking in order to make the most of those last few metres when the car is travelling at its maximum speed. The advantage in terms of cornering speed will certainly be greater.

On modern Formula 1 circuits it is common to have a succession of bends not linked by any straights. The idea when tackling a chicane of this kind is to concentrate on the last bend and sacrifice the early ones. In the illustration, the car indicated by the continuous line is wide on entry and tight on exit in the first right-hand bend, in order to take the second bend as effectively as possible and accelerate early on exit, whereas the driver of the car following the dotted line is obliged to delay the moment when he can accelerate and regain speed.

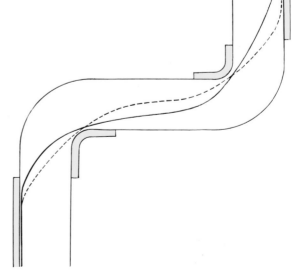

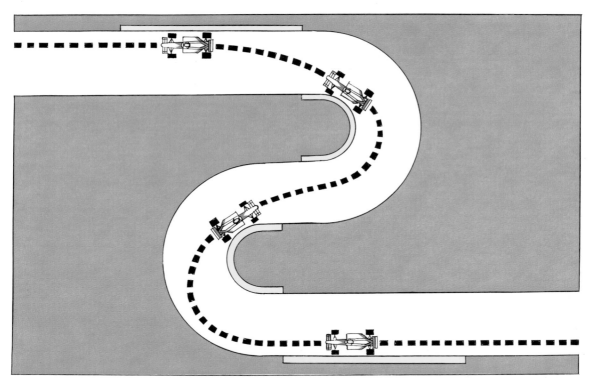

This illustration shows the application of the rules which have been explained so far. The racing line is planned to achieve the best possible exit from the second hairpin. This means taking a wide line on the entry to the first bend in order to be in a better position to tackle the second. Although he has sacrificed the first bend and increased the time it takes to drive through it, the driver is in a position to accelerate early and approach the following straight at higher speed. As can be shown, the old rule of 'slow in, fast out' is always valid.

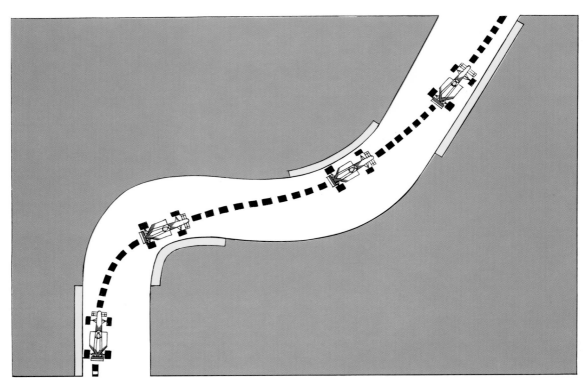

This is a chicane where it is the exit which must take priority because it is a fast bend. The driver sacrifices the first right-hander by going to the kerb very late: in this way he will find himself in a position to attack the second left-hand bend at higher speed. The illustration shows this situation, which is not uncommon on modern Formula 1 circuits.

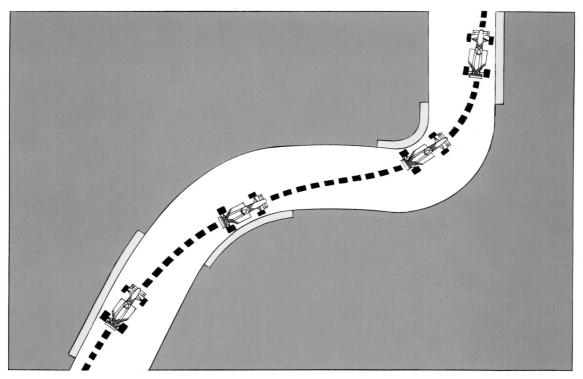

In this case, on the other hand, you must give priority to the first part of the chicane because it is the first corner which is the fast one, while the second is slower. The driver will hold a straight line until the second apex, keeping his speed up as much as possible. You should brake just before the second bend, which will then be tackled with a less favourable line.

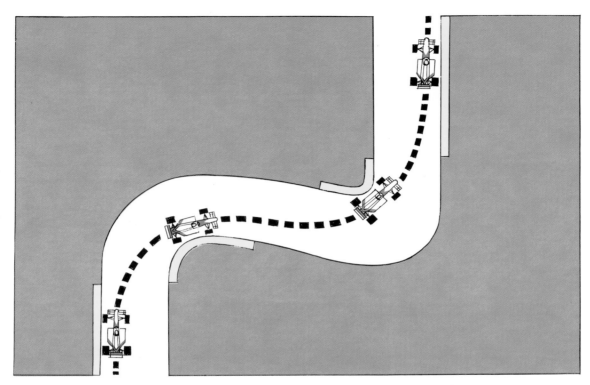

In taking this chicane, the driver must sacrifice the entry so as to exit faster. This style of driving is dictated by the length of the straights which come before and after the chicane rather than the layout of the bends. The illustration on this page is an example of when the longer straight is immediately after the chicane.

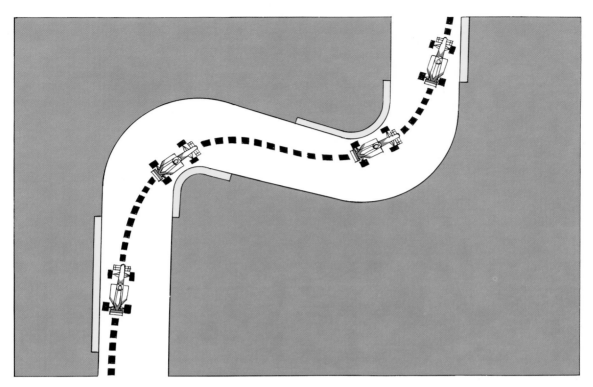

In the illustration above we see a chicane which comes after a long straight. In this case the driver must compromise the second half of the chicane so as to lift off and brake as late as possible and thus lengthen the straight. In so doing he will come to the left-hand bend too near the inside kerb and on the exit he will have to wait to have the car straight before he can start accelerating.

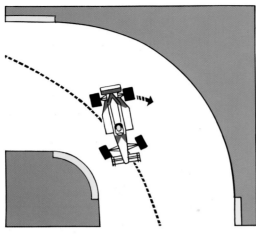

Oversteer. The front of the car grips and holds its line while the rear has a tendency to widen to the outside of the bend. There are two kinds of oversteer: power or deceleration. The first is caused by excessive wheelspin, the second by the absence of traction (that is to say rear-wheel grip) and the subsequent increase in drift. This behaviour will always cause the car to 'wiggle'.

Understeer. The rear grips and holds its line while the front runs wide. Understeer will slow a car down less than oversteer and this is why many drivers set the car up so that it is slightly understeering on fast bends. Understeer can be caused by a lack of grip at the front or by too strong a push from the rear wheels: this situation can be a constant one or be caused by outside factors.

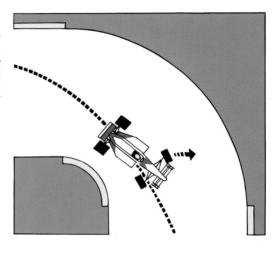

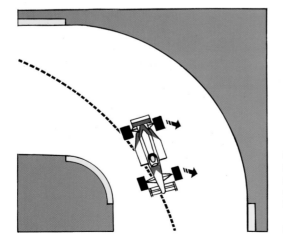

The four-wheel drift (or controlled skid). The front of the car and the rear increase their drift simultaneously and the car slides towards the outside of the bend with all four wheels in a line. The steering wheel is straight and the driver controls the car with the throttle (rear wheels) and the steering (front wheels). This technique was often used with the cars of the 1950s and 1960s and is still found in rallying. It can be used in medium-fast bends.

Chicanes are where the fate of a race can be decided. Created in order to slow down Formula 1 cars, they require hard braking on entry and violent acceleration at the exit. If we sacrifice the first bend in favour of the second we can exit faster from the latter. This picture was taken at the first chicane at Monza.

CHAPTER 3

CORNERING: CONTROLLING THE CAR

There are two means by which a driver controls his car: the steering wheel and the throttle. The first controls the front end, the other the rear end. To describe what a driver has to do more effectively we divide the bends into two fundamental groups: slow and fast.

Slow bends have to be taken with the technique of advancing the cornering phase, as we have seen for the hairpin. As the first part of the racing line involves a bend with a very narrow radius, the driver will have to try and turn the car as fast as possible in order to be in a position to get back on the throttle without delay.

In this he can be helped by the car's set-up, which, depending on the settings, can be more or less 'nervous'. Normally this is how we describe a car that has a tendency to oversteer. Thus, after braking, which in this case will be late, the driver will have to turn in sharply (but without putting the car into a spin) and wait to accelerate. The car, slowing down thanks to engine braking and centrifugal force, will start to drift, taking a bigger radius than the bend itself. At this stage the driver must not touch either the steering or the throttle, and will only be able to do so when he reaches the exit line and is ready to gain speed once more.

Then he will have to accelerate and at the same time straighten the steering wheel. If the car should still drift, the driver will have to apply opposite lock – quickly but with restraint. Speed and precision are fundamental to this type of 'salvage' manoeuvre. The

Pages 50-51: *The McLaren shown in this picture has a balanced set-up. The front wheels are following the radius of the bend, neither turned in too much (understeer) nor turned out too much (oversteer); they are nearly parallel to the white line. A balanced car allows a driver to set himself up for the next bend without too much trouble.*

most common mistake is to overdo the opposite lock: this will produce a sudden change of direction and oversteer from the opposite direction. This secondary oversteer is much more dangerous because it is more immediate and violent, and requires a second application of opposite lock – more difficult as the wheels are usually turned a lot further.

In the case of a slow corner, but one that is wider than a hairpin, you have to take the same actions knowing that when a car drifts while decelerating you can continue to make it slide by increasing the power suddenly: this is power oversteer.

For fast bends the best set-up is one tending to understeer. Firstly because it is more controllable given the speed, secondly because it slows the car down less than oversteer. Entering a bend, the movement of the hands on the steering will have to be very delicate, the opposite to what is needed for slow bends.

The car must never be left decelerating because the speed would magnify the tendency to oversteer: if the car starts to go from the rear end, never lift from the throttle, or there will be a ruinous spin. Acceleration will have to start before, or at the same time as, the turn-in. If the car has been given a neutral set-up, it will hold its line up to its limit of grip, when it is best to have understeer for the reasons explained above. Understeer, like oversteer, is controlled with the throttle: as you decelerate, the effect decreases and the front end finds grip again; as you accelerate, it is increased, with the front wheels having even less grip.

It is a mistake to lift off the throttle completely and decelerate violently: if this happens you could experience a sudden shift from understeer to oversteer.

For all kinds of bends the following fundamental rules apply. The line must be set up at

the entry, the first part of the corner, then everything follows naturally. The less you turn the steering wheel the better, avoiding unnecessary movements and corrections which will take you further from the proper line; the ideal set-up is a neutral one, but once the limit of grip is reached, on a twisty circuit it is more convenient to have a touch of oversteer, while on a faster track it is best to have understeer. In a slow bend oversteer can be controlled with the steering, while understeer in a fast corner is rectified with the throttle.

At some time during a race you will have to widen your line at the exit of a corner and use the whole width of the track. You can do this when the kerbs are not too high, as here at Silverstone, when it is not raining and when there isn't any grass on the outside. In these cases we must expect to bottom out, with the underside of the car touching the ground.

Today's Formula 1 drivers, from the front of the grid to the back, are all brilliant drivers. The difference between them no longer lies in an original racing line or the proper set-up. The days are over when on the same bend you could see six or seven different racing lines. These days, the 'X factors' which can lead to success, apart from the ability to go easy on a car, are braking and gearchanging. The driver who has a car which is not outstanding can't make up the time in the corners, since everyone takes them perfectly and there is only one racing line, but will have to do it by braking as late as possible, and by changing gear as fast as possible.

On a racing track braking must always be very decisive, even if the surface is slippery, as in the case of rain. Brakes on a Formula 1 car are designed to perform at particular temperatures: anyone who fails to reach them will have less efficient braking. On a dry surface, braking can even be violent, because the rule is to brake as late as possible and the later you brake, the more aggressive you have to be. Braking on the limit may cause one or two wheels to lock, depending on the level of grip, and that can result in the car going into a spin.

Either way you lose time, because soft-compound tyres (race tyres) deteriorate quickly when the wheels lock. This in turn leads to a loss of precision in your driving as well as a shortage of grip due to a lack of balance. At best your lap times will increase, but more typically you will have to return to the pits and change all four tyres. This is because once it has been 'flat-spotted' a tyre has a tendency to lock under braking.

The nearer the limit you lift off and brake, the better. There are no precise rules: braking is the aspect of driving that requires the most physical effort and practice if it is to be executed perfectly. It isn't just a question of courage: above all you need to be aware of the limits of the car and of the circuit. This is the only way to brake consistently on the limit yet with a certain degree of safety, without having to think constantly, 'I wonder if I'll get out of this . . .'

To exit a bend while accelerating and exerting maximum torque, you have to be in the right gear. The best time to change gear must be while braking. The actions of braking and changing gear are closely connected. After the start of the braking sequence, you should wait a little before changing gear, so as to avoid over-revving. Here too there are no precise rules but in my experience it is wise not to change down before you have travelled at least a third of the length of the intended deceleration zone. And while changing down – double de-clutching, of course – it is also important not to reduce the intensity of your braking, because apart from the danger of entering the bend too early, there is a risk of over-revving, even if you have waited the right amount of time in the decelerating phase.

If you have to tackle a tight bend after a long straight, dropping, say, from sixth to second, in theory it is not necessary to go through the gears: many drivers brake, change gear, and then blip the throttle to keep the engine revs up. Of course, on a slippery surface (when it is raining, for example) going through the gears will help to keep the car balanced and avoid the risk of locking the back wheels.

An old rule has it that you should brake only when you are travelling in a straight line. It is a rule that is still valid today, even if it is not as inflexible as it once was. The reason braking should take place, for the most part, in a straight line is the transfer of weight within the car when braking, cornering and accelerating. When a single-seater is beginning to decelerate, there is a weight shift from the rear to the front. If we assume an initial weight distribution of 40 per cent at the front and 60 per cent at the rear, it may change to 75 per cent at the front and 25 per cent at the rear. This weight transfer (35 per cent) is very useful as it gives extra grip to the front wheels which are under more stress while braking. If this happens on the straight, there is no problem, but on a bend this force will apply at an angle to the car's direction of travel.

In the case of a right-hand bend, for example, the weight transfer happens from right to left, reducing the weight on the inside wheels. While braking on a bend these two weight transfers operate together, with the result that the inside wheels may lock because they experience the same braking force as the outside wheels, but without the same load and therefore with less grip. Despite this the sensors fitted to Formula 1 cars show that a number of drivers do brake on bends. Thanks to the very high levels of grip from today's cars, this can be done in safety.

While it is not possible for the naked eye to see the weight transfers that affect a Formula 1 car, we can think instead of a heavy saloon which goes into a fast corner which tightens on the exit: the effect is the same, even though in a Formula 1 car it all happens in the few millimetres which the suspension allows.

In the case of rain, or if the surface is less grippy, the weight transfer from the rear to the front is much less (15 per cent) than when the tarmac is dry. By keeping the same braking force you run the risk of locking the front wheels because, while the braking force is the same, the load on them is less. Thus you have to alter the distribution of the braking effort, and the way to do this is by using the brake balance control in the cockpit which can be adjusted by the driver even when he is racing.

Using the brake balance control you have to switch some of the braking force from the front to the rear, which will be loaded more because less weight is transferred to the front. In this way you will have an effective and balanced braking action on the four wheels, all equally efficient as the braking load has been evenly distributed.

This will be indicated by an even braking pattern on all four wheels; if, on the other hand, the front or rear wheels lock while braking on a straight, it means that the force is not evenly distributed.

CHAPTER 5

ACCELERATION AND GEARCHANGING

As we have already indicated in the chapter devoted to braking, these days it is possible to overtake an opponent using acceleration and gearchanges. Technicians and race engineers are always searching for extra horsepower, but if the driver does not make the fullest use of his engine, the technicians' work is wasted.

The driver, even though he is not an engineer, must know the fundamental parameters which characterise an engine: these are power, torque and revs. They can be summarised in a graph which allows the driver to understand the characteristics of the engine he is dealing with. Power is the indication of the 'strength' of an engine, and is achieved at a precise number of revolutions, which is usually different from the maximum the engine is capable of: it is normally slightly lower. Here we confront our first problem: do we take the engine to its maximum revs or do we limit ourselves to reaching the engine's maximum power?

An old-fashioned engine tuner would answer: accelerate as long as the engine continues to pull. As we reach the power limit we could change up, but it is also true that engine revs produce speed, especially when we are racing with conventionally aspirated engines (remember those frantic races with the engines revving at 13,000 when the turbos were dropped?).

As always the best solution lies between the two extremes, particularly when we consider that the values for peak power and peak revs are not that far apart and that the chance to achieve another hundred revs is always useful.

Knowing an engine's torque curve is fundamental if you wish to exploit it properly. It is important to know that the engine must always be used within a band in the rev range

Because of the rigid suspension on a Formula 1 car, the chassis comes under great strain on fast bends and when accelerating, as this picture shows. The inside front wheel is off the ground, and therefore has no grip as all the weight is on the outside wheels. A driver must bear this in mind when he is accelerating.

extending from the point of maximum torque to a point between maximum power and the maximum allowed. It is in this band the engine performs best, and this is linked to the driveability, or flexibility, of the engine.

An engine is said to be flexible if this band is of 2000 or 3000 revs. More usually the band in which an engine is still pulling and has torque is about 1000 revs. It is worth saying that if you allow revs to drop below the point of maximum torque, you are lost. Knowing these parameters and their relative values, a driver can get the most out of his engine in acceleration because he knows his power band and the maximum number of revs at which he must change gear. When you reach this maximum number of revs you have to change up. It is an everyday action for anybody who drives a car, repeated hundreds of times. And this is what beginners think, bothering only to avoid crunching the gears, not realising the advantage that a quick gearchange can give. Experienced drivers will always gain something when they change gear, and if this advantage seems minimal (a few thousandths of a second), once multiplied by all the times that you have to change to a higher gear it adds up to quite an advantage on the clock. There isn't only the loss of time involved in the gearchange itself, but also the 'dead' time in which the engine cannot push the car. This dead time, equivalent to a dab on the brakes, is felt more at high speed. The ability to change gear quickly is not a skill that a driver needs to be born with: luckily you can learn from experience. It is also true that with today's semi-automatic gearchanges these skills are on the way out, because with these systems the gearchanging time is the same for everyone (assuming the same gearchange system, of course, which shifts everything onto the technological plane). With these systems there are two distinct advantages: the gearchange is faster than with a manual gearchange and the driver does not have to take his right hand off the steering wheel, thus increasing safety and his capacity to control the car. But to get back to the traditional gearchange: the worst mistake is to over-rev. A hundred revs are enough to shatter a Formula 1 engine.

There are four situations which will cause an engine to over-rev. The first happens on the straight, at the time of a gearchange: the driver keeps his foot on the throttle too long and goes over the rev limit. To avoid this simple mistake (yet imagine there's a group of you, a few inches from each other and it's the first few laps: who has the time to look at the instrument panel?) engineers fit rev limiters, which effectively cut the electrical supply when the engine reaches its maximum.

The second situation is when changing down before a bend. The downshift involves a double de-clutch and a heel-and-toe, and for this reason the less able drivers may be preoccupied with the execution of the manoeuvre and pay too little attention to braking. Thus, when the foot lifts from the clutch pedal, the engine has not dropped down in revs as it should, the car will suffer a violent deceleration (which if too hard may lead to a 360-degree spin) and the driveshaft will be overstrained. This is the most common and dangerous type of over-rev because the rev limiter cannot cut in as the engine is moved by the wheels' inertia.

Of course over-revving is not only down to driver error. The brakes might fail or the driver might experience fading brakes, lap after lap, so that he has to use the gears to slow the car down. It is an emergency operation, which can work when the speed is not too high, but the engine is almost always damaged.

It is possible to over-rev exiting a corner as well as at the entry. The driver, intent on using every available inch of the kerb or – in the early laps of a race – worried by what the car in front is doing, may not notice that he has reached the rev limit and keeps his foot hard down on the throttle. This too is very common, but at least here the rev limiter can cut in and warn the driver to change gear.

But the most brutal and the most ridiculous way to over-rev the engine fatally is to miss a gear on a straight. This is how it can happen. You take your foot off the throttle, press the clutch, the right hand looks for the gear, and hesitates while the right foot floors the throttle, dramatically increasing the revs – more than usual because the engine is not connected to the gearbox. Usually a driver will realise in time, but sometimes it's too late. Another way of making the same mistake is to select a lower gear than intended. If this action is followed through to the end, serious damage to the engine and transmission is inevitable and the risk of a 360-degree spin is very high. Usually, though, with a certain kind of sensitivity which you can develop over the years, the driver realises he's made a mistake just as he is doing it. Even though he has kept his foot on the clutch, the car will hiccup, and the driver must understand what is happening and take appropriate action.

This response is purely instinctive, and its effectiveness depends on our reflexes. Both these mistakes are usually due to tiredness, which leads to loss of concentration. They are not caused by lack of driving skills, but by excessive physical stress which can also lead to mental stress.

The torque and power curves of a modern Formula 1 engine. It is essential for a driver to be familiar with the torque and power curves for his engine if he is to make full use of it.

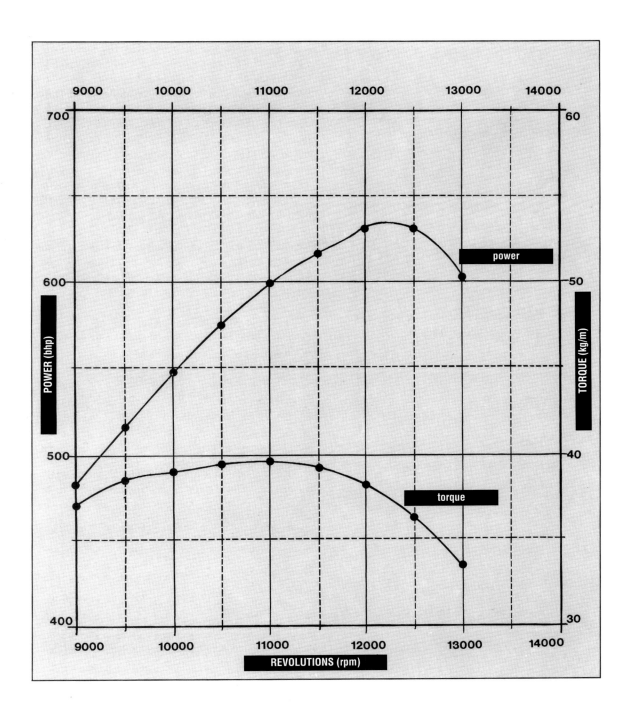

CHAPTER 6

MAKING THE BEST USE OF YOUR TYRES

The aim of a driver and his team in setting up the car is to ensure that the tyres operate in the best possible conditions. Only in this way will a tyre, which is one of the fundamental components of a Formula 1 car, perform to the limit of its potential. The parameters which govern a tyre's performance are its pressure, and the temperature of the carcass and of the top layer of rubber.

All decisions regarding tyres are taken jointly by the driver, the technical director, the team manager and the representative of the tyre manufacturer.

The right pressure is necessary to maintain rigidity and prevent temperatures rising. A driver will immediately notice if a tyre is under-inflated because it will squirm when loads are brought to bear; this will lead to an increase in temperature and a loss of grip. In Formula 1, all you need is a difference of 0.1 bar to ruin the performance of a tyre, and the only time the pressure is deliberately increased is when there is heavy rain: the rounded shape given to the grooved tyre in this way will help expel the water.

The temperature of the tyre, at the surface and internally, together with a visual analysis, provides a measure of its condition and performance. Each tyre performs best at a given temperature which must be reached at all costs, but you must not go over it otherwise the tyre will perform less well. These operating temperatures are provided by the tyre manufacturer and teams try to keep to them scrupulously. Each time the car stops the tyres are checked – in the middle and on both sides of the tread, about two millimetres below the surface, in order to obtain a complete picture of the tyre. Only by doing this and by comparing the data from the front and back wheels will the engineers know how the tyres are operating.

Pages 70-71: *The kind of tyres used in Formula 1. The left-hand one is grooved and is for rain. The other is a slick tyre, used in the dry. Both are available in qualifying trim, that is with special compounds designed to enhance the car's performance. These tyres last only a short while and perform at their best for only a few laps.*

The reading taken is an average of the temperatures of the carcass and of the surface of the rubber (which is why readings are taken with the needle laid at an angle and not vertical, so as to have a larger testing area). There should not be a great difference between the two temperatures (the carcass is usually cooler than the surface); if there is, the top layer of rubber will slide and make the tyre drift more.

The driver should notice this himself, feeling the car drift more and more in each successive bend. The engineers in the pits will be aware of it from the rise in tyre temperature and the formation of ripples, evidence that the top layer is gradually moving towards the outer edge of the tyre. The reason for this is likely to be a lack of balance between the front and the back of the car. At this stage you have passed beyond the ideal situation, where the tyre produces its best performance and wears evenly – something you can even spot on television, when you can see that the tyres are shiny and evenly worn.

In the pits they know the tyres of a car out on the track are in good condition when the driver does a fast lap. If he does a whole series of them, it means the set-up is such that it allows the tyres to remain close to the ideal temperature. Usually, when a tyre has reached its peak, it then starts to overheat, lose grip, and wear unevenly and excessively. The reaching of this point, when the tyre deteriorates noticeably, depends on how good the set-up was. It also depends on the type of tyre: naturally a qualifying tyre will not last more than one lap (and at times, if the driver has accelerated too fast on the warm-up lap, not even that), while the harder race tyres can comfortably survive the 300 kilometres of a Formula 1 race.

The warm-up lap during official qualifying,

Checking tyre temperatures: in Formula 1 this is a critical operation because it provides data for the race engineers on the car set-up and the level of grip of the tyres. Tyres play a crucial role in a single-seater's performance: a good car fitted with the wrong tyres is unlikely to win a race.

when you break the tyre in and bring it up to the correct temperature, is very important: if a driver doesn't warm it up sufficiently, for example, he will not have good grip in the first few bends of his fast lap, and as a result will not be able to set a good time.

During a race, when the driver realises his tyres have passed their performance peak, he must ease his pace a little (if the race situation allows) or, if a tyre change is planned, exploit to the full what the compound still has to offer.

The next stage after 'rolling' (when the top layer of rubber slides on the tyres' surface) is the formation of blisters on the surface of the tyre. This may be due to overheating of the surface compound or to the excessive temperature of the carcass. From the cockpit, the driver will see irregular stripes on his tyres, which is how the blisters appear at speed. At this stage you must stop at the pits, because when the blisters burst (and it does not take long) the tyre is considered unuseable.

Obviously if during the course of a race a tyre gets to this point, the work undertaken by the engineers in the preceding days has been to no avail. But it might also mean that the driver has failed to make proper use of his set of tyres, perhaps getting involved in a fierce battle in the opening laps, when the car is laden with fuel. A good driver must never make this major tactical error during a race.

In this picture we see Ayrton Senna checking a report on the tyres fitted to his McLaren. The choice of tyres is of fundamental importance to getting a good result, especially when you are after pole position. In order to find the right set, the engineers turn into alchemists, swapping compounds from one side of the car to the other and from the front to the back.

CHAPTER 7

BEYOND THE LIMIT: ACCIDENTS

I n order to make me aware of my limit as a driver, and of those of the car and the circuit, an old mechanic, in the days when I was karting, said to me: 'When you feel that the road is escaping you, when you say to yourself, "That's it, I'm going off," but then instead you stay on the track, that's when you've reached your limit; you've gone as fast as you could.' This is the best definition of being on the limit that I have heard in my driving career. To get to the limit and then drive on it is like being on the edge of a razor: very few can do it.

And it's not something that can be learned that easily: acrobatic talent is a gift you either have or you don't. In many people's eyes a driver who has learned certain things with experience will always be an artificial driver, while someone with natural talent will be a champion. And this is the difference between the two: champions attempt seemingly crazy manoeuvres and stay on the track; the others rarely get away with it. Most stay below the limit, then suddenly attack a bend, go beyond the limit of grip and have an accident. Taking the whole driver/car/track equation, it is much easier to go beyond the limit than to drive on the limit.

So let's look at the causes of the accidents that most commonly result from overstepping the limit.

An accident can end in two ways: with the car going off the track or with a spin (which may end beyond the edge of the tarmac). Leaving the track is obviously worse than spinning. One of the most common mistakes which leads to going off is to put the front tyres on a 'dirty' part of the track. This can happen when overtaking in the wet (or in the dry if it is a circuit where the racing line is limited), or when a back-marker is being lapped in a corner and has to move onto the part of the circuit where the cars don't usually go. It happens quickly and unexpectedly, and the driver rarely has time to adopt a defensive strategy as there is no warning. It is also a bad accident, as it usually involves the front end, the most vulnerable part of the car, and puts the driver's legs at risk.

In this type of accident it is wise, a few moments before the impact, to take the hands off the steering wheel and place them on the shoulders, crossing your arms in front of your chest: that way you will avoid breaking your wrists. This is the only situation where it is advisable to take both hands off the steering wheel. A spin, on the other hand, is foreseeable, because the car, to a greater or lesser degree, depending on how it is set up, will warn the driver that he is about to lose control, giving him a chance to react. You may spin under braking, because too much braking effort is concentrated at the front end, or because rain has led to an imbalance in the car. It can happen in the middle of a bend, caused by excessive speed. And it can happen exiting a corner, too, a mistake typically made by novices, who, out of enthusiasm or because they have got their racing line wrong and wish to make up the time they have lost, apply the throttle more fiercely than the level of grip offered by the road surface or the conditions will allow.

It is much easier to spin as a result of using too much power at the exit of a bend when driving in the wet. But you can also spin like this because you have climbed up on the outside kerb a little too much. It may happen, for example, when you overtake on the inside on medium-fast bends: as you have had to advance the apex, you will be on a wider line at the exit. On the kerb the tyre has less grip because cement has less grip than asphalt and because kerbs have irregular sur-

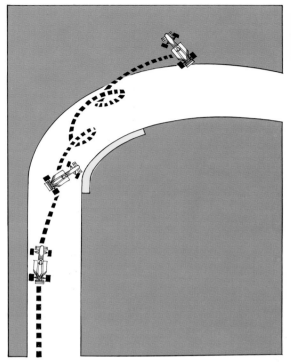 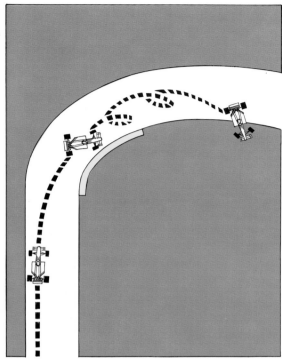

When a spin leads the car to leave the track on the outside, it means that the loss of grip has happened before the bend's apex. To compensate you have to apply opposite lock at the start of the spin. Then, holding the steering wheel steady, you must brake firmly in order to slow the car down as much as possible. By braking, you will have a better chance of keeping the car on the circuit because you will increase the spinning radius.

If a car starts spinning, it tends to stay on the line it had before the driver lost control. Thus when a single-seater loses grip after the apex, it will leave the track on the inside of the bend. This spin – unlike the first one, which can be caused by too much aggression – is the result of a driving error, such as excessive determination in catching a spin or a drift. It is a mistake frequently made by beginners.

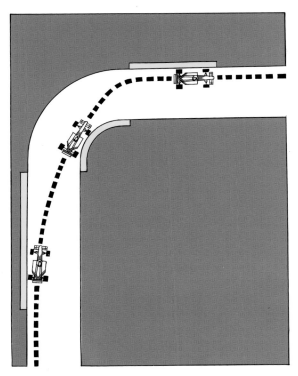

In the event of a mechanical problem while braking, or while approaching a corner, you must try and reduce your speed as much as possible so as to make it easier to find an escape route. To do this you have to start steering much earlier and let the car go straight towards the outside of the track without checking it. You have to take your foot off the brake – not an instinctive manoeuvre – and turn the steering wheel to straighten the car only at the last moment.

faces. And because they are painted, they are always to be avoided when it rains. Even in a very nervous car, one that is stiffly sprung and does not give much warning, a spin can always be felt by a driver who has the ability to anticipate and driving sensitivity: you apply opposite lock, and if it is done fast enough the whole thing can be reduced to mild oversteer.

Here too the difference between the top driver and the journeyman can be seen: the latter is always late and regularly ends up in the fence. If it hasn't been possible to straighten the car, as soon as the driver feels it go, he has to start a damage limitation exercise. It is the same for a motor cyclist: once he has lost control it is useless and dangerous to try to hang on to the handlebars in the hope of restarting more quickly. Thus a single-seater driver must not persist with the opposite lock once he has realised that he is going to spin: to do so will take him off the track and will lead to a much more violent shunt.

There are a series of rules which must be adhered to rigidly in these instances. Firstly you must press the clutch pedal in order to keep the engine running and prevent the gearbox and drivetrain being damaged when the wheels start spinning in the opposite direction. If possible, it's also a good idea to keep the foot gently on the throttle too, so as to avoid being unable to restart. I did say 'if possible', as it is not easy to keep accelerating while you have your foot hard on the brake. The wheels must be kept locked until the car stops spinning as that will reduce speed and make the circles wider, increasing the chances of the car staying on the track (which will allow you to restart). While braking and keeping the engine revs up, as you might during a tyre stop, you should make no attempt to steer. Once a car starts to spin, you must not move your hands on the wheel (and of course under no circumstances should you take your hands off it!) as the damage might be much more than otherwise.

Only at the end of the spin, when 80 per cent of the energy produced by your speed has been absorbed, can you attempt to correct the course of the car to allow it to stay on the track. It is a matter of luck, of course, but only in this final phase, when you recover control of the car, is it possible to attempt a reaction. You must also bear in mind that the car will find grip much more quickly after a spin in a fast corner, which happens at high speed. These can be dangerous accidents because they happen quickly and at high speed. But if the driver is tenacious, has a little talent and a little luck, he will come out of it, partly because as the bend is wider the chances of staying on the track are higher.

The one time a good driver goes over the limit on a systematic basis is on a qualifying lap. It is well known that the big risks have to be taken in practice and not in the race: in a race you should always be slightly below your limit and the car's. Drivers who always drove on the limit – and were adored by the fans – were the exception to the rule. On a qualifying lap, or in practice, when you have to find the limits of the car, there are usually more accidents. This is why practice sessions require at least as much concentration as the race itself.

Accidents can happen, and the important thing is to ensure that no injury results. In this respect modern Formula 1 cars are vastly superior to those of the past. The photograph captures the instant before Ayrton Senna's McLaren overturned in the 1991 Mexican Grand Prix. The car skids at the entry to a corner, spins and slides towards the gravel trap. Before stopping, the car overturned.

CHAPTER 8

DRIVING IN THE WET AND IN DIFFICULT CONDITIONS

A circuit is not always in a perfect state, with the right kind of grip and no undulations. In truth it happens very rarely. Most of the time we race on an old surface, full of bumps, which disintegrates as soon as the Formula 1 cars pass over it. It has to be repaired overnight, and then comes apart again in the morning, because it is impossible to rebuild a track evenly like this. Or, when the track is near the sea, between one session and the next, the organisers have to have the circuit swept as the wind has brought sand onto it. And then you have the situation that is adored by the public: the race in the rain, a modern-day bullfight.

What is good is that the changing track conditions affect everyone, so that everyone starts with the same handicap. Then it's up to the individual to make full use of his experience and natural ability, which are particularly apparent in these conditions. First, let's consider a dirty track, with the 'marbles', which reduce the grip available. This example applies to all difficult track conditions except for when it rains. As the cars take more or less the same racing lines, a sort of pathway forms which is the only clean part of the track. Drivers have to keep to it, and not deviate by more than about 10 centimetres, or the result might be an early exit. There is no way round this problem, except to rely on your intuition (and to luck when overtaking).

Circuits with a very uneven surface are a special case. The car is under great strain, but what's worse is that the suspension and the aerodynamics are unable to follow these sudden changes of level. This makes the driving of sensitive cars very difficult, because the reactions are not the usual ones. The car has to be set up for this uneven surface by raising it from the ground so as to avoid it bottoming out. It has been calculated that bottoming out

Monaco Grand Prix 1991. When the track is dirty with sand, debris, oil or whatever, it becomes hard and tiring to drive, just as if it were wet. You have to be very careful not to go on the 'marbles', the areas where the dirt collects. Particular care must be taken on street circuits where the Armco barrier is close to the track: to touch it is fatal.

at 300 km/h results in a speed loss of 3–4 km/h, which is equivalent to losing 20 bhp!

Rain changes everything, because the loss of grip does not happen as suddenly as it does on a dirty track. Thus you have time to make corrections, turning the steering wheel gently and avoiding sudden movements of the brake, throttle and steering wheel. Braking must be extended to the point where the wheels start to lock. The foot must lean on the pedal and press it progressively to this point. If the wheels do lock, you have to ease the pressure on the pedal, then start braking again. The throttle and the gearbox too must be handled less violently than when the surface is dry. While changing gear, for example, the clutch must be eased out slowly to allow the rear wheels to engage progressively without spinning.

In the rain your lines through the bends must be altered to avoid the areas of least grip, the parts of the track where the water is deepest (because of track unevenness or because the bend is slightly banked), and those that have become covered in rubber due to the constant passage of the cars. These are obviously on the normal racing line. When it is dry rubber on the surface allows more grip (though it does depend on the surface temperature and the amount of rubber that has been put down), but in the wet the same line becomes treacherous, because the water brings rubber residues to the surface, creating a layer which is not fixed to the asphalt. Thus it moves and is very slippery. As soon as the tyre traverses an area like this, it loses much more grip than if there were water alone. This is why the wet racing line is so different from that taken in the dry.

First of all while braking we will have to stay at least a metre from the outside kerb, to avoid the black line left by the loaded rear tyre. Braking will be a little longer and that will mean crossing the line normally taken at the entry of the corner. If before we went to brush past the kerb at the apex, now we will stay well away to avoid an area where there is bound to be lots of surface rubber. This is why we say you should 'stay wide' in the rain. At the exit we join the dry racing line, which at this point inevitably coincides with the wet one.

These are not fixed rules: the method adopted to tackle a bend in the wet varies from driver to driver and from bend to bend. Some, who favour a more aggressive driving style, can take the inside line, as they feel comfortable putting the car sideways, while others, who have a neater driving style, will opt for the outside line.

The result may be the same, but clearly a driver with a neat driving style in the wet has more chance of finishing the race. A classic example of this is provided by the Parabolica at Monza: to take the normal line and brush the kerb in the wet is tantamount to risking a spin (because the front wheels are turned more), and means using a lower gear than if you follow the outside line. The difference in exit speed is visible even to the naked eye. The areas of acceleration in the wet are substantially the same as in the dry; what changes is the way you accelerate: you must not be violent, but always decisive and progressive.

After very heavy rain, maybe the next day, the track, though dry, will not permit the sort of speeds possible before the rain. The reason is that the water has washed away all the rubber, so the road surface is fast but lacking in grip. In this case it's best not to be among the first out on the track during qualifying so as not to help the other drivers by laying new rubber down.

The first to go out on the track at a Grand Prix are the drivers from the smaller teams, or the drivers who need more time to set their cars up, while the last are always the top drivers, who battle each other for fractions of a second till the last minute.

Rubber on the track is a difficult area to handle. For example, the compound that has been laid down must be compatible with ours, otherwise our tyres may pick up some of the rubber on the track which will alter the handling, or they may slide on the incompatible compound. Temperature is also important, because if it is too hot, and there is a lot of rubber on the track, it will melt and will not provide grip. You have to consider each situation in isolation, bearing in mind the way the surface will affect the grip of your tyres. A problem we cannot seem to solve, such as understeer in the middle of a bend, may be caused by an excess of rubber on the track, or by incompatibility with our own compound.

If it rains, and there is time to alter the set-up (but that is not always the case), there are a few tricks which can help adapt a car for the wet. The first of these is to soften the suspension to allow the car to lean more and thus reduce the stress on the rain tyres, which are grooved. We must then soften the shock absorbers, reduce the rate of the springs and reduce the diameter (or the position, depending on how it has been built) of the roll bar. Some even have it disconnected, so as to increase the rolling effect of the car. These changes enable the car to turn into the corners more effectively and allow the driver to feel the car more, which in these conditions is no bad thing. Of course, a car that has been set more stiffly in the hands of an expert driver will, in 90 per cent of cases, be faster. On the aerodynamic side, we have to put on more wing front and rear. We need to increase the load on the wheels by pushing the tyres against the ground in this way to avoid the risk of aquaplaning.

Tyre pressures will also be changed if it rains, being increased by 0.1–0.2 bar. This is done to make the area of the tyre in contact with the track rounder so as to help the water run off along the grooves. We have already mentioned the changes to the brakes, while for the gears it is wise, as the speeds are lower and acceleration less sudden, to reduce the ratios. It is also important to note that in the wet it is unnecessary to hold the gears up to top revs, but it is best to use longer ratios which put less pressure on the tyres. Of course all this is done when we have time to do it. Otherwise we run the car set up for dry conditions, only modifying the aerodynamics and tyre pressures, as they take the least time.

The driver too must prepare himself for driving in the wet. The visor must be sprayed externally with a water-repellent solution which will make the rain run off, and internally with a demisting solution. You can also fit removable layered visors, especially useful in the first few laps, or when the field is closely bunched, to get rid of the oil leaked from the exhausts of the cars in front.

A driver's boots must be absolutely dry before he climbs into the cockpit. If you have no one who will dry them for you, don't be ashamed to put plastic bags over them. The gloves become very important in the wet because they can be used to clean the visor. If this doesn't work, some drivers have tried racing with a chamois leather stitched to the forearm of their overalls, and this seems to be effective.

The start is even harder when it is wet than in the dry. This is because visibility, especially for those who are behind the first

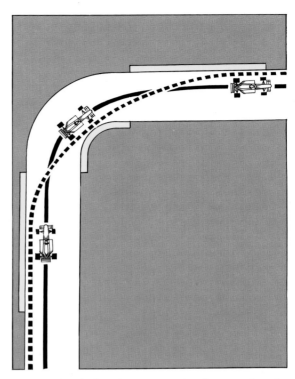

When racing in the rain or on a wet surface, you have to change your racing line. When braking it is best to stay at least one metre from the kerb; in the middle of the bend, instead of aiming for the apex, you take a slightly wider line, where there is less rubber.

two rows, is practically non-existent. There is therefore a big risk of running into the back of another car, especially under braking. To avoid this it is a good idea to check the landmarks you have previously noticed in practice out of the corner of your eye, as well as moving out from behind the car in front on the straight to see what is going on.

In the race, if the rain stops and the surface begins to dry, it is wise to look for the puddles on the straights and drive through them in order to keep the rain tyres at a slightly lower temperature to lessen their deterioration.

It goes without saying that you have to be very careful when overtaking, because the only drying line is going to be the one used by everyone. Everywhere else the water will clear much more slowly and it will remain slippery much longer.

Driving in the wet demands a mixture of precision and delicacy. The lines you take are nearly always different from those used in the dry. Even though modern tyres guarantee previously undreamed-of levels of grip, acceleration and braking in the wet must still be done carefully. Especially while exiting a bend, it is important to know how to feather the throttle to avoid unnecessary oversteer.

CHAPTER 9

TESTING AND THE CAR'S DEVELOPMENT

A driver's job is not limited to racing and qualifying laps: even though many modern Formula 1 teams have a test driver, the racing driver must take on the boring and demanding task of development testing throughout the season.

This involves hundreds and hundreds of laps, all at the same speed, to establish whether the right choices have been made; full Grand Prix length tests in order to check reliability; tyre testing organised by FOCA, or by the tyre manufacturers themselves; and tests on the circuits on which we will race, essential to find effective race set-ups and to continue the development work on the car.

The life of Grand Prix driver knows no rest between March and November. And it isn't easy work. It's not enough that he covers all these laps with consistency and reliability (the speed goes without saying), but he must also be analytical, identifying the best solutions and sharpening his instincts so as to tell the team and the engineers the reaction of the car in the different set-ups.

If a driver is not able to do all this, his season, which may have started with a new car which has potential but needs to be developed, will gradually worsen while others improve. If all goes well, he might strike lucky, but that is all. But over a season, and over a career, these flukes count for little, and he will be remembered as a second-rate driver.

The tests planned by a Formula 1 team at the start of the season are of two kinds: those which will allow a car to be properly set up for a particular circuit and those seeking an overall improvement in the car. The first are, in the majority of cases, connected to the qualifying sessions and untimed sessions which take place before every race. They are essential to allow the driver to adapt the handling of the

The photo shows Ayrton Senna in the McLaren garage shortly before going out onto the track. The tyres are warming under the covers, and the mechanics are ready to fit the bodywork. In a few minutes the car will be out on the circuit to set a qualifying time, and we will know whether the decisions made by the team of engineers and tyre specialists were the right ones.

car to the circuit. If the necessary compromises between the parameters which govern the performance of a racing car are not found, often due to unforeseen breakages or accidents which slow down the development programme, we won't do ourselves justice and will be reduced to a supporting role. In other words we will not have a good race. The second type of testing is intended to increase the car's potential. These sessions are the longest, where the driver and race engineers test the new solutions developed by the technical staff on the basis of information gained on the track. Without proper development testing a car will never reach its full potential and, as the season progresses, the gap to the top teams will steadily widen.

More than ever before, it is essential to be able to develop a car which may not be outstanding, instead of having a car which shows great promise at the start of the season but then lacking the organisation or the programmes to improve it. In addition, the chances of finding a good set-up in pre-race testing are largely dependent on the amount of data the team has on the car and its handling.

Testing is a little like preventive medicine (the last word, of course, belongs to the stopwatch): it allows us to speed up our work and concentrate on the very important, in fact fundamental, honing of the machine.

Ayrton Senna keeping track of his times and those of his opponents on the monitor. A driver's job is not only made up of racing and qualifying; he must also shoulder the duty of testing and developing the car.

CHAPTER 10

A DRIVER'S NATURAL TALENT: TO BE A GOOD TEST DRIVER

We have seen that it is not enough for a Formula 1 driver to be fast: he must also possess the rare quality of being a good test driver. There are a whole range of gifts a driver needs to become a champion. Nature does not usually bestow them all in one place: one driver receives some, his rival others. Occasionally, however, a true champion emerges who embodies all the qualities of the perfect driver: statistics indicate it happens every ten years or so.

It is because they lack these qualities that so many honest journeymen are kept out of Formula 1; they are what the talent scouts are looking for in the young drivers racing in the lower formulae, as they search for future champions and seek to link them to their team, perhaps as part-time test drivers.

These qualities are: driving talent, driving sensitivity, the capacity to anticipate, technical know-how and the right mental and physical attitude. Of these, the first three are gifts a driver receives at birth or in the formative years, and time can only refine them. The last two, however, are the fruit of experience. There have been drivers who became World Champions without these five qualities: luck is sometimes capricious on whom it bestows its favours. As the saying goes, you become a driver, but you're born a champion.

A driver with talent will be fast from the very beginning of his career; he will have a talent for recognising the most effective racing line, and the limits for braking and acceleration, he will instinctively know, without being told, how to make use of the whole track. The youngster who will become a champion is easily recognisable because he has an instinctive mastery of many of the fundamentals of driving which others have to be taught. In later years he will have to be lucky enough to find experienced, objective teachers to help him hone his natural driving abilities.

To be a sensitive driver means analysing the car's reactions through a bend, feeling the effect of different set-ups – in other words, understanding the car. This too is a natural talent which can't be taught and can only be sharpened by time. If you do not possess this quality, you might become a very fast driver, but never a test driver.

To be able to anticipate, to foresee the car's reactions, is a considerable advantage. The only way to exploit this natural talent is by establishing a reference system based on everything a driver absorbs concerning racing lines, acceleration and braking. Operating within this system, which aims to make driving methodical and ordered, a driver can tell when something is amiss. In order to take full advantage of his ability to anticipate, a driver must always be in top physical and mental condition because that is the only way he will remain calm and lucid, even in unforeseen situations.

Take, for example, a car which slides too much in bends and suddenly snaps into oversteer. Having the ability to anticipate means feeling the car go an instant before it does, and preparing appropriate corrective action just as the car is about to start sliding. A driver who does not possess this quality will feel the car only when it has started to lose grip, and in most cases correction at that stage is futile. And the same can be said of braking which causes us to overshoot, or violent acceleration. It is all about sensing what is about to happen an instant before it does, because there has been an interruption of our search for points of reference. So being able to anticipate means looking beyond what you are doing at any given moment.

In the case of a bend followed by a straight, a driver who knows how to anticipate has already crossed the apex as he is entering the corner; at the apex he will have glanced at the kerb his outside wheels will mount as he is exiting the bend; and when he reaches the exit, in his mind he will be looking for the points of reference for the next bend.

Only by applying himself in this manner will a driver never be overtaken by events. To have the ability to anticipate does not necessarily mean having fast reflexes. Reflexes are a neurological reaction of the nerve centres to a sudden stimulus. To anticipate means acting before something happens: it is not a reaction, but a true action.

If a driver has a certain amount of sensitivity, he will become an invaluable asset to the team in setting up and developing a car. He will be able to describe the car's behaviour in the most accurate and detailed manner. Then the engineers will decide what adjustments and modifications to make on the basis of the information he has provided: this is why it is important for a driver to be in a good team.

But if you are aiming to be a complete driver, capable of overcoming the shortcomings of a team which might not be of uniform strength, you will also have to have a solid technical grounding, so as to be able to voice your opinion when new solutions or set-ups are discussed. This is something which great champions have, because to be able to suggest new solutions to your race engineer is an indication of a very special talent. The difference between a good test driver and a World Champion is that the former is content to report the car's reactions, while the latter, drawing on his experience, can also suggest changes that might be made and rule out ideas that would not be beneficial.

The last quality which a modern professional racing driver must have is to be outstandingly fit and mentally well balanced.

Because of the ever-increasing stresses imposed by the cars these days, a driver might waste the work of months just because his physical condition will not allow him to finish a race, or might cause him to lose composure – and that half-minute that cost so much effort. Like technical knowledge, physical fitness is something you acquire with time and effort. And nowadays you have to be an athlete not only to be Formula 1 World Champion, but even to win a single race.

But if the importance of being physically well prepared is obvious, mental preparation may seem less decisive. But that is not so, because before being a racing driver, you have to become a man. If that does not happen, it does not matter how much talent you might have, you will never reach the top, because for one reason or another the results which might seem within reach will continue to elude you. We will talk about this at greater length later.

CHAPTER 11

HOW TO INTERPRET THE CAR'S BEHAVIOUR

A driver has to tell his team of technicians about his car's reactions, so he needs a certain amount of sensitivity, but he must also be able to interpret and explain its behaviour. Let's see what a driver must know so as to give a clear and concise account.

The first thing to learn is how to divide a bend into three sections: entry, middle phase and exit. The second is that bends divide themselves into two major groups: slow and fast. There isn't a league table to classify slow and fast bends, we have to analyse them circuit by circuit. For example, on a track with a high maximum speed, say 280 km/h, a so-called slow bend will be taken at 140–160 km/h. On a very fast circuit, with an average speed of 250 km/h and a maximum of 340, a bend can be considered slow even if taken at 200 km/h.

In the lower formulae, a slow bend is one taken at less than 120 km/h, a speed at which aerodynamics do not play a part. Formula 1 cars reach that speed in second gear, with mid to high gearing, and the only bends taken in first are the hairpins, which are not considered slow bends, but starting points for acceleration. The entry to a slow bend is a test of a car's cornering ability, its liveliness. In this situation you get the best performance with a car which has slight oversteer at the limit, because that way it corners better, is more responsive to the steering and generally makes us waste less time both at the turn-in point and at the exit.

In the middle section of a slow bend, the car will be sliding with the rear if the speed is very low, or will already be accelerating if the bend is a little faster. If the car is decelerating you have to assess how much the rear end is drifting, while if you are already accelerating you will have to consider the traction of the rear wheels.

Exiting a slow bend, the car will be accelerating hard, so it is important to concentrate on the traction you have at the rear. In other words, you must see if your set-up will allow you to put the power down when you need it and in the amount required.

Entering a fast corner, the car is already accelerating, the amount of throttle depending on the bend. Our focus, in contrast to a slow bend, must be on the front end because in this type of corner the ideal car is one that understeers slightly when it reaches the limit. Thus it is the front end that allows it to remain on the right line.

In the entry phase we will have to make sure that the front tyres do not lose too much grip through excessive understeer, as this would lead us to lessen the pressure on the throttle and therefore lose speed. In the middle of the bend, the car's weight is completely on the outside wheels. You must find the balance between both ends of the car, watching out for understeer, oversteer, or a four-wheel skid. In each of these cases we will have to find maximum lateral grip and a neutral set-up. At the exit you should feel slight understeer; this is the best way to exit the bend at top speed. Here too, as on the entry, you will have to concentrate on the front end, checking that the understeer is not excessive.

If you do not find these characteristics in any of the three phases of a slow or fast bend it may mean that the car is set up wrongly: then you have to start all over again. It may be that you simply want a different set-up to suit your driving style with a car that is pronounced in its oversteer or understeer, but it could also be that you have wrongly interpreted or affected the track behaviour of your car.

If the desire for a particular set-up is something that emerges late in a driver's career, at any rate when he is an established professional, the other two situations are very common, especially among those who are just starting to race. A thing that novices must watch out for is not to influence the set-up of the car with driving errors that result in misleading information for the team. If, for example, during the opening laps, when brakes and tyres have yet to reach their optimum working temperatures, you lift off and brake a little earlier, you will reach the middle of the bend at a slower speed than usual and that will naturally prompt you to accelerate earlier. This will probably lead the car to understeer on exit but, as we have seen, this behaviour is related not to set-up but to driving style, and changes to correct this 'false' understeer will affect the proper set-up.

Another example is that of the excessively aggressive driver, naturally inclined to lift at the last moment. This style requires sharp movements with the steering wheel and slightly later acceleration than usual. In this case the car will be more likely to oversteer, but here too this will not be caused by the set-up.

Another classic mistake is to confuse cause and effect. A typical case is when oversteer at the exit is caused by understeer at the entry. If the driver does not recognise this link he will want the oversteer corrected while instead the problem is the understeer. Because the car slides away at the front end, the driver thinks he is not steering enough and increases the lock to counteract the understeer. When he has reached the steering limit, which is reached quite quickly, by turning the wheel further the driver will have the opposite effect: oversteer. This is because he has braked the rear end of the car with the front wheels. At this stage the game is up and the car will slide out of the bend on its rear tyres.

From this it is obvious that a good driver, and a good test driver, is one who is conscious of what he is doing and, above all, has total confidence in his handling of the car.

CHAPTER 12

SETTING UP THE CAR

In motor racing, including Formula 1, you must always reach a compromise between the various settings which affect the performance of the car. There is no clearly defined procedure that will allow you to find the most effective set-up in a scientific and dependable way.

Even experience, fundamental and necessary as it is, can have its limitations as each situation is new and individual. A small change in temperature, a little more rubber on the track, or a few bumps which weren't there before can be enough to create a new situation.

A good test driver must know the areas of the car that can be modified in order to enhance performance, because one day he will have to call on those skills. These changes are substantially of two kinds: mechanical and aerodynamic. Until wings appeared at the end of the Sixties the possible adjustments were mechanical. Today aerodynamics are of predominant importance and it is here that most development takes place.

In order to have a good aerodynamic set-up, you have to start from a sound mechanical base. This is why you set up the car mechanically on the slow bends first, then aerodynamically on the fast ones, before coming back to consider the mechanical settings in relation to the new aerodynamic set-up and adjust the wings for the slow corners which, as we have seen, are rarely taken at less than 120 km/h, the speed at which you begin to feel aerodynamic effects.

The mechanical parts on which the engineers work are the suspension, the differential and the ride height. As far as the suspension is concerned, they alter the stiffness of the springs, the settings of the shock absorbers, the size and material of the bump-stops, the size of the anti-roll bars, and the angles of the wheels and the suspension, such as the camber, toe-in and toe-out, and castor.

Alterations to the springs, shock absorbers, bump stops and roll bars are meant to regulate the way the car handles, and thus the load each wheel must bear. Nowadays we do a lot of work on the bump stops, while pre-loading of the springs was given up about three years ago. Given the limited travel of a Formula 1 suspension, we work above all on the bump stops, which regulate the movement of the suspension once it has reached the end of its travel. With soft bump stops, the suspension will harden progressively, while harder bump stops will load the wheels less.

The angle of the suspension (castor) and wheels (camber, toe-in and toe-out) are adjusted to influence the movements of the wheels. Castor (or the angle of incidence of the upright) offers three very important characteristics: straight line stability, predictability in corners, and the tendency to straighten the wheels after a bend. For example, on a track with big, fast corners, the castor will have to be pronounced, giving the driver heavier steering, stable at high speeds. On a twisty track, the steering will have to be lightened to avoid tiring him. The second factor affected by the castor angle is the load on the inside wheel when steering: exploiting this can make the car turn more easily.

Camber is the angle at which the wheel is inclined, and is of fundamental importance in ensuring that the tyre has the best possible contact with the track. Nowadays the wheel camber angle is always negative, and its value changes according to the stiffness of the sidewall of the tyre: the stiffer it is, the less camber will be necessary.

Toe-in/toe-out (alignment) helps control the angles of the wheels when the car is moving, and by altering it you can increase or decrease the car's cornering ability. Together with the steering mechanism, wheel alignment is critically important in a single-seater racing car, even if nowadays – because the amount of roll in corners has to be limited in order to avoid altering the lower and upper profiles of the bodywork and reducing the footprint of the tyres on the track surface – it is modified only to increase the immediacy of the steering.

An important feature of a Formula 1 car is the capacity to vary the percentage of locking of the differential. It is often used to correct the car's behaviour in the middle of a bend, when the amount of drive from the rear end is of crucial importance (a reduction in the level of locking produces increased grip from the rear wheels).

Changes to the ride height alter the load brought to bear on the front and rear axles. Raising the front end of the car, for example, will reduce the load on the front wheels and increase that on the rear wheels when you need to cure oversteer. But the increase in ground clearance means that more air will pass underneath the car and ground effect will therefore be less efficient. This example shows how important it is, when working with the settings on a Formula 1 car, to reach a compromise, objectively weighing up all the pros and cons.

Aerodynamic alterations are limited to changing the angle of inclination of the front and rear wings (when it is increased the wheels are loaded more heavily), or modifying their shape and profile. The working principle is very simple, but there are so many variables that a driver cannot hope to master the subject and has to rely on the aerodynamicist in the team. Aerodynamics offer a two-edged sword: more wing provides increased grip in the corners but means more drag on the straights and thus less speed. As ever, you have to judge each situation on its merits. At Monza, for example, a lot of downforce allows us to take the two Lesmo corners and the Parabolica faster, but costs us quite a lot of speed on the straight.

In the case of oversteer the car will generally have to be softened at the rear to increase the load on the rear wheels: you could also modify the camber of the rear wheels (the negative angle may have been too great, resulting in a small footprint) and the front wheels (very little negative camber, so the tyres grip too much), the wheel alignment at the rear (too much toe-out, leading to difficulty holding the racing line) and the front (too much toe-in, which brakes the rear wheels). It is also possible to work on the settings for springs, dampers and front roll bar, hardening them, so as to lessen the grip of the front tyres and balance the two ends. In the case of understeer, the opposite will be done. Soften the front end and, if necessary, stiffen the rear; camber will be reduced at the front and increased at the rear, as will toe-out.

As far as aerodynamic adjustments are concerned, in the case of oversteer, you have to increase downforce at the rear and decrease it at the front; the opposite applies if the car is understeering. But if the team cannot find the right set-up, it can work on the characteristics of the tyres, with softer or harder compounds. An understeering problem that cannot be solved may be fixed by fitting softer tyres at the front. It may not be the best way to exploit a car's potential, but it has helped a driver more than once.

CHAPTER 13

THE CHOICE OF GEAR RATIOS

A Formula 1 driver has the task of choosing the right gear ratios to match the length and characteristics of the circuit. The idea is to find the ratio which will allow you to complete the full length of a bend without having to make a further gearchange, which would be a risk if the car is heavily loaded, and would in any case waste time. Thus the driver must select the ratio which suits the bend perfectly, finding a compromise if the circuit's characteristics make it necessary. For example, having sorted out three-quarters of the track, we come to a bend where, if we take it in a certain gear, say third, we are forced to change up to fourth before it is completed, obliging us to depress the clutch and thus lose rear-wheel traction just when the car needs it. It is a risky situation which, on the other hand, gives us more stability and increased acceleration leading to the next gearchange.

However, to take the bend in fourth, something you must always try, means that when we want to accelerate we will find the engine at low revs and thus with less torque. The disadvantages are a loss of time in acceleration, less stability while taking the bend and less engine braking while braking. The advantage is that the car enters and exits the bend at higher speed, even if it takes longer to pick the revs up.

If you cannot make further alterations because the rest of the circuit is all right, you have to be guided, as always, by the clock, choosing the solution which costs you the least time over a complete lap, bearing in mind that the longer ratio helps the engine's reliability and always guarantees a higher exit speed.

You start by settling which ratio will allow you to achieve full revs at the end of the main straight. It is important to select this ratio accurately because a reduction of 200 revs at maximum speed results in a significant loss of time. Once it is settled, you work downwards, seeking the right ratio for every bend. The only proviso to bear in mind is that the drop in revs as you change up from one gear to the next should be progressively reduced as you work your way up through the gearbox. This is because the longer ratios used at high speed will not allow the revs to rise as quickly as the shorter ones.

This is why it is easier to find the right gear in the case of a bend that is taken at moderate speed: if you have to shorten a ratio in order to exit a bend faster, it's best if it is first or second gear. The choice of first gear – which is used to take off at the start and is then used in the tight bends, such as hairpins – is also important. If there are no hairpins, the choice of first gear depends solely on the start and, once chosen, taking into account the characteristics of the engine and the driver's preferences, it can be retained for all the races where the starting grid has the same features.

Ratios are often altered between qualifying and the race, because the car's performance will be reduced and it will be heavier, with the tanks full of fuel; ratios are also changed if the wind increases, and they can be lengthened if a driver is not starting from the first two rows of the grid and the track allows slipstreaming: in this way we will have more speed than our adversaries at the end of the straights and will be able to overtake them more easily.

CHAPTER 14

THE WARM-UP

After the final qualifying session, on the Saturday, the driver and the engineers meet to decide the race set-up. In other words they are looking for the optimum compromise (tyres, aerodynamics, settings) which will allow the car to reach its potential not only for a lap, but for the whole one-and-a-half-hour race. The only opportunity to check the decisions which have been taken and even make some changes is in the Sunday morning warm-up session.

Usually, cars lap with an 80 per cent fuel load on board, sometimes on full tanks. The huge differences in lap times which sometimes occur can be explained by the different amounts of fuel carried. And differences between two drivers in the same team may have less to with driving styles than with the set-up of their cars. The team manager, together with the drivers, may decide to give one car, for example, a faster aerodynamic set-up and softer tyres and the other more wing and harder tyres. Apart from the times set during the warm-up, it will be reliability for the duration of the race which will decide which is the best solution.

During the morning session the driver must not overdo it, must not look for fast times, but make sure the car works properly and that the choices made are the right ones.

A few inexperienced or excitable drivers have had accidents during the warm-up, negating the work done in the previous three days.

Ayrton Senna's McLaren is pushed out of the garage to start the warm-up. These final tests, last-minute checks on the performance of the car, and the tyre and aerodynamic choices that have been made, are undertaken on the morning of the race. In these tests you must never overdo it, nor look for great results; just make sure that everything works as it should.

CHAPTER 15

THE LINE-UP AND FORMATION LAP

Before the start of the race the cars must move onto the grid and take the places allocated to them after qualifying. They come out of the pits, go round the circuit once and line up ready to start. This lap is also useful for the teams to check whether there are any oil or water leaks or whether a tyre is losing pressure. It is the last chance to make sure that everything is as it should be.

Once this lap was more important because it was used to bring the tyres up to their operating temperature (or as close to it as possible in so short a time) and to bring the pressures up to the level required for the duration of the race. The use of tyre warmers has changed this because they help bring tyres to their correct temperature (and at the right pressure).

When the drivers have taken their places on the grid, the engines are kept warm until all the cars are ready. At this stage the grid is peopled only by team members, journalists and photographers. Five minutes later everyone is cleared from the grid, the engines start up again and the race director starts the formation lap with a green flag.

Notwithstanding the manner in which each driver chooses to focus, at this stage the race has begun, in the true sense of the word. This is when the drivers must bring the tyres up to the right temperature, then the water, oil and brakes. To do this they will have to manoeuvre the car violently, which will also increase their confidence in their mastery of the machine.

It is not easy to warm a racing car to perfection in a single lap. It is easy to fall into one of two diametrically opposed errors: either to stress it too much or too little.

It's always best to have a firm hand, but without overdoing it: if you have a spin, or leave the track and stall the engine, the race will be over before it has started: and that is not a pleasant experience.

During the formation lap – and this is something you learn quickly in the lower formulae – the driver must also leave his mark on his opponents, let everyone know he is not there to be pushed around, that he will finish as high as he possibly can. A squeeze on a bend, a hint of overtaking, a braking manoeuvre extended to within a few centimetres of the gearbox of the car in front demonstrate your intentions and ambitions: these feints and thrusts are a sort of declaration of war.

The driver in front of us, who may not be perfectly mentally and physically tuned, might actually start the race with his eyes in the rear-view mirror, losing sight of the cars ahead of him. And that is a fatal mistake: if this is how he has started, in most cases he will be easy to swallow up later.

1

The starting procedure continues after the formation lap. Approaching their starting position on the grid, the drivers will try a practice start, to clean the tyres and increase their temperature, and then try some hard braking, in preparation for the first bend.

When all the drivers are lined up, a marshal will walk across the track behind the last two cars waving a green flag to indicate the race can start. The race director will now show the five-second board, which means that

2 **3**

the red light may come on at any time during the five seconds after the signal is given, and around four seconds after that the green one, to indicate the start of the race.

On the subject of the red and green lights, it must be said that many drivers used to count to four from the moment the red light went on and then start (and some still do). In this way they had a small advantage, even of a few tenths. However, the time between the two lights is not fixed, but can vary slightly at

The start of a Grand Prix, Canada 1990. As the lights go green (1), Ayrton Senna, number 27, is first off. Gerhard Berger, number 28, starting further back as he was second fastest, crosses over the track (2 and 3) and tucks in behind Senna's McLaren. This will allow both McLaren drivers to take the first bend well clear of their rivals.

the discretion of the starter. This trick is
therefore very risky, and it can lead to an
accident or a ten-second 'stop and go' penalty
(the punishment imposed by FISA on those
who jump the start).

The drivers who start halfway down the
grid, where they are less closely observed, can
move to the right or to the left in order to dart
between those in front of them more easily.
As for the positioning of the places on the
grid, one of the two columns will be on the
side of the track where the cars don't usually
pass: the track here is dirty because it is off
the racing line. If you find yourself in this situation it is a good idea to clean this section up

by passing over it with your car during the Sunday morning warm-up, even if this means departing from the usual line.

There is no need to emphasise the importance of a good start. It can transform a situation which might have seemed hopeless on its own, just as a poor start, perhaps because of a missed gearchange, can drop you back from the first couple of rows to the middle of the grid. It is not only the immediate consequences that make a good start important. On a short and tortuous track like Monte Carlo it's vital to start well because of the difficulty of overtaking; on a fast circuit, where slipstreaming is important, such as Monza or

A wet start requires great reactions and a delicate touch on the clutch and throttle. This is the 1991 San Marino Grand Prix at Imola: once more Ayrton Senna is first off the mark and frees himself from the curtain of rain thrown up by the wheels of the other cars. In starts of this kind the drivers further back are at a disadvantage.

Hockenheim, staying in touch with the front-runners is half the battle, because once a driver is left behind and loses the slipstream, he will have great difficulty in catching the leading bunch who are pulling each other along, in the way long-distance cycle racers do on the long flat stretches.

Once he is on the grid, the driver knows that the race will soon start, but he must not yet select first gear. He will only do that when he sees the five seconds sign. Then he will depress the clutch and ease the gear into first, checking very carefully, by easing out the clutch, that he is in the right gear. It becomes immediately apparent by the amount of resistance offered by the pedal. This fundamental check will only edge him forward one or two centimetres, not enough to affect his position.

It is important not to engage the gear too early: the clutch, which in just a few moments will come under intense pressure, might overheat. Once the gear is engaged, the driver will have to rev the engine. We are not talking about boy racers taking off at traffic lights, and the driver should keep the rev count constant and fix his eyes on the red light. There are two reasons for this. Firstly, the engine is always at high revs, whereas if he plays with the throttle the light could turn green when the revs are going down; secondly, he should look at the rev counter only at the outset, then the eyes must be on the red light, so as not to get caught out while looking at the rev counter.

The engine must rev just under its limit, which allows for a quick response and the possibility of increasing the revs if needed. At the green light, the driver must let the clutch slip, so as to balance the theoretical speed corresponding to the engine revs with the zero velocity of the car on the grid.

Slipping the clutch is the most important

and difficult aspect of the start. It must not slip too much because it might burn out and the race could be over on the spot, and in any case the wheels would not turn, as you are accelerating too hard while the clutch is not yet fully released. But it must not slip too little as this may cause you to stall the engine (very dangerous on the starting grid) or make a poor start by jumping forward, which could even damage the differential. In both instances the start will be slow as the ideal is to slip the clutch in a way that allows the car to take off in the shortest time possible. It is

This is what can happen at the start on a narrow circuit with an early bend. This is the first rush towards the Casino after the green light at Monte Carlo in 1991. Gerhard Berger brakes late in his McLaren, the wheels lock (note the black marks), and he is passed by the other drivers.

preferable to let the clutch slip a bit less, as a burnt clutch almost always means the end of the race. Once the car is in motion, the left foot leaves the clutch pedal and the focus moves to the throttle. Now it is vital to reach the right number of revs to engage second gear as soon as possible.

In a perfect start the wheels will hardly spin, the car will quickly be up to speed and will be in second gear very quickly. If the acceleration has been too fierce, however, the wheels will spin, creating a lot of smoke, and the car will gain revs but not speed. The driver must be aware of this, because if he

A start accident which has become famous: the Japanese Grand Prix 1990. The photo on the left captures the moment of contact as the sparks surround Ayrton Senna's McLaren and Alain Prost's Ferrari, the other shows the exit of both cars. Start shunts of this kind happen quite often as the cars are entering the first bend. This is where the danger is greatest.

changed gears his engine would lose power. Thus, in a situation of this kind, he must ease the throttle so as to find grip again. In this stage of the start the driver is largely dependent upon his sensitivity and experience.

As he can't look at the rev counter (in the opening laps, as at the start, it is not wise to take your eyes off the track and the other competitors), the driver must be aware the engine is revving too fast or that the time has come to engage second gear by listening to the engine and interpreting the vibration he feels within the chassis. On the subject of changing up, it is always better to do it a moment too early than a moment too late: that is the way to avoid a guaranteed over-rev.

The start and the opening laps must be approached with great determination. A driver must not wait for things to happen, but on the contrary he must act first, creating a situation which may be to his advantage. Only with this spirit, the winning one, can a driver hope to make a name for himself and gain good results, although he must avoid the mistake of being over-aggressive. But it isn't always easy to start so aggressively.

One way is to imagine the outcome of the start, the approach to the first bend, how to force his opponents into a mistake, where to overtake them. While doing this the driver can visualise the start of a perfect race, with maybe two or three alternatives, so as not to be demoralised if things don't work out as imagined. Thus, when he is on track facing his opponents, he will be reacting to images he has already seen, and his reaction time will be shorter. This technique is used by the majority of drivers both because it is effective and because of the peace of mind it gives at the start: you have the impression of not having to face something unknown and of knowing (although only in your imagination) what is going to happen. And there is quite a difference between starting blindly and knowing what will happen.

This is another reason why you have to qualify well: starting from behind means a long uphill struggle and that is, of course, much more tiring. When taking their racing line the drivers in front tend to close the door on the ones arriving behind by taking the inside line. Usually overtaking happens on the outside because, with the tendency to 'close' a bend by being in the middle or even on the inside of the racing line, a bottleneck forms on one side of the track which allows the following drivers to come through. This is important for those who start in the third row of the grid or even halfway down.

The approach to the first bend and the first few laps are, as we have already said, all to do with instinct and timing. On a race track, whilst fighting alongside other drivers, it isn't possible to take the eyes off the circuit in order to check the instruments like the rev counter, a distraction which could lead to an accident.

As at the start, you have to drive by the seat of your pants in the next few corners and even on the straights, changing gear when you feel the time has come. This is something that can be learnt, you just need a modicum of mechanical aptitude. But it is also essential to proceed with caution, because a mistake due to inexperience, caused by a lack of reaction from the driver, can be disastrous. It has happened in the past and it seems too high a price to pay for a moment's carelessness.

This illustration provides a schematic view of the line-up of the cars at the start of a Grand Prix. The crowding in just a few metres of track is remarkable, and this image helps us understand how difficult it is for a driver halfway down the grid or at the back to make a fast start.

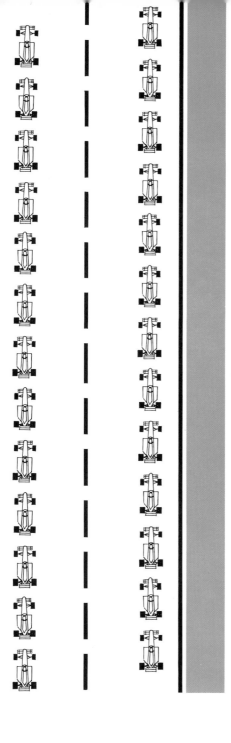

The start on a street circuit bordered by concrete walls. This is the United States Grand Prix at Phoenix, Arizona. Ayrton Senna is first off the mark and Alain Prost in the Ferrari (number 27) is trying to take him on the inside as the first bend is a right-hander. On street circuits in particular it is just as well to leave the crowd behind because shunts are very common.

Overleaf: *This is the next photograph in the sequence. Ayrton Senna, first away, turns into the first corner followed by Alain Prost, who we saw previously aiming determinedly for the inside to avoid being overtaken by the other cars. This picture shows the problems you may face if you start from the middle of the grid.*

CHAPTER 17

THE OPENING LAPS

The two most dangerous moments of a race are certainly the start and the approach to the first corner. This is not only because all the cars are so close to each other, but also because the drivers are not acting rationally but are relying on their instincts. From the second or third lap on, when the race has settled down and the pack has thinned out, the driver will start to weigh up his actions before putting them into effect.

As soon as you start, the energy repressed by your concentration frees itself, exploding in a series of actions repeated dozens of times, carried out automatically. Alessandro Nannini said in an interview that he never remembered anything about the start and the first two laps. Although this varies from one driver to another, it is quite true.

Approaching the first bend, the driver will do the usual things: brake, change gear and select his racing line, always conscious of the cars in front of him. The only one who will be able to set up the bend as he wants, braking at the last moment, will be the driver who is first into the bend. He will have the advantage of being able to brake a little later than usual because, starting from the grid, his entry speed will be less than when he arrives in full flight. The drivers behind, on the other hand, will have to brake earlier because of the bottleneck which forms at the first bend: the driver who is last will be the first to brake. This is why, although they were so close on the starting grid, after the first few laps the gaps between those who started at the front and those halfway down the grid are already huge.

In order to make up lost ground and overtake a driver who has been quicker off the mark, you have to apply constant pressure to make him understand that you are intending to overtake. This is done close up and requires great determination. Here Ayrton Senna is putting pressure on Alessandro Nannini in a Benetton.

CHAPTER 18

OVERTAKING

The point of a race is to finish ahead of everyone else. If we find ourselves behind someone our aim is to overtake him; and if we are in front of someone, our aim is to avoid being overtaken. Either way, a race round a circuit is synonymous with overtaking. Once you reach a certain level, the performance of the drivers and the cars is fairly similar. Thus the first thing to learn is that only rarely can you overtake because your car is more powerful than your opponent's.

Instead there are a number of factors which are linked to the driver: we can overtake if we have tackled the previous bend better than our rival and we have come out of it faster, if we have braked better at the end of the straight, if we have led him into a mistake or if we have risked everything and closed our eyes hoping for the best. The driver must actively create chances for overtaking and pressurise his opponent into a mistake. This duelling is the real fascination of Formula 1 races.

A successful overtaking move means you have studied your opponent and discovered his weaknesses. And in order to identify them, we have to stay behind him a for a few laps before attacking him with determination.

If, for example, he exits a corner badly, we may leave him some room in order to attack him better without being slowed down by his car. In this way we will have made up the gap and will exit with more revs. And if there is a short straight after the bend, then it's done: at the end of the straight, or at the latest as he is braking, we will have gone in front. If instead his problem is in entering the bend, in braking or in setting up the racing line, we

In this picture, which shows Ayrton Senna in his McLaren ahead of his team-mate Gerhard Berger, we see the way a driver positions himself behind the car he is chasing to take advantage of the slipstream.

could overtake him in these phases, outbraking him and forcing our way onto the inside line.

If the driver in front, knowing that he is slower on this bend, chooses a line which tends to hug the inside, we may decide to go for the outside. This was once the preserve of the true champion, but today, thanks to the superior machinery, we see people succeeding even in Formula 3.

There are two situations in which it is impossible to overtake on the outside: a very tight bend, like a hairpin, and a chicane. In the first case we don't have the time to overtake the other driver whilst on the outside of the bend: at the end of the corner he will accelerate and, as he will still be in front, he will have no difficulty reaching the outside kerb first, forcing us to slow down. In a chicane it is impossible to pass on the outside because there is only one possible line and no escape route: if we are in trouble we can either brake and get back into the slipstream, or go straight on, if we are on the limit; otherwise we risk an accident. It is obviously better to stand on the brakes and renew the chase, but this is not always possible.

Our opponent may not tackle a big sweeping bend correctly: in this case, on the exit, we can slipstream him and, if the straight is long enough, overtake him with the help of the slipstream, as described in the next chapter. If you manage to get alongside the car in front at the time when you're lifting off, obviously on the inside of the corner, in effect you have already overtaken your opponent. There is no need to crush him psychologically and pass him by the whole length of the car, and that way there is a risk of overshooting. It is sufficient to catch him and be alongside him, maybe a metre ahead, just enough to prevent him from closing the door. Now we are in

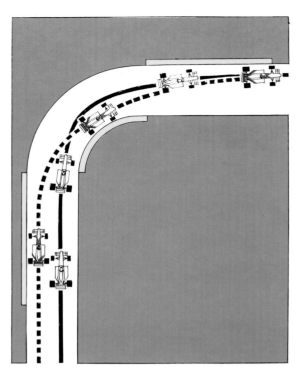

This is the typical attack under braking. The car following the continuous line has attempted to overtake, but has not managed to come up beside the other car. So the car on the dotted line has closed the door and forced the other car to brake hard, forcing it to miss the apex and exit onto the straight in a weaker position.

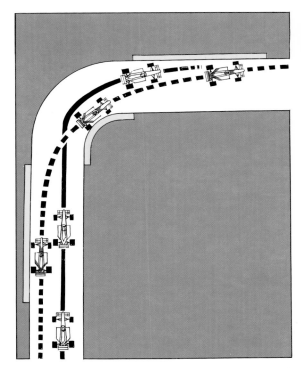 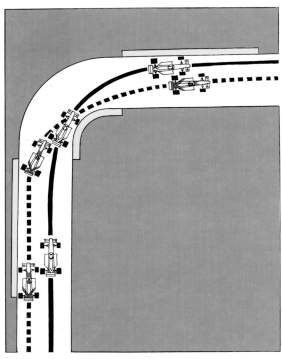

The driver on the continuous line has braked late and must concentrate on keeping the car on the track in the middle of the bend, and will then have to take a wide line, which will slow him down. The driver who has been overtaken stays wide while braking and tight on exit so as to try and get his position back on acceleration: this spectacular manoeuvre is often successful.

The car on the continuous line has completed its over-taking manoeuvre, but the driver on the dotted line has not given up and tries to get his position back. This manoeuvre does not always work, because the driver who is in front can delay accelerating or might take the centre of the track at the exit: the speed and direction is up to him.

front and, as we have not overshot, our rival will not be able to retake us on the inside once we have come out of the bend.

If, on the other hand, we do overshoot the mark, we will have to advance the apex and take a wide exit: in this case he will regain his position, overtaking us on the inside at the exit of the corner. Or, if we have arrived at the corner too fast, we find ourselves in the middle of the track, intent on keeping the car on the road rather than regaining speed. In this case too, because of the speed differential and because our rival has kept to the proper racing line, we will be overtaken on the next straight.

There is a way of avoiding being overtaken in both these instances. If you have overshot on a wide radius curve, get back to the apex and then stay in the middle of the track at the exit, so as to shut out the opponent; or, if you have entered the bend too fast, accelerate a little later than usual so as to slow down the following car. It may not be the most sporting way to drive, but in some instances, for example at the end of a tough race, or when a podium place is at stake, these thoughts are dwarfed by the desire to win.

In order to overtake an opponent we can also push him into a mistake: a missed gearchange, accelerating at the wrong point, misjudging a line. When we see one driver overtaking another with ease on television, it is often the case that the one in front has made a mistake, and the one behind is reaping the benefits. But if this mistake – which in F1 is never too obvious – were to happen suddenly, as a result of a lapse in concentration, the pursuing driver would probably not manage to overtake. Instead he puts pressure on his opponent, keeping close to him and feigning attacks with the aim of making him lose his composure and pushing him to make

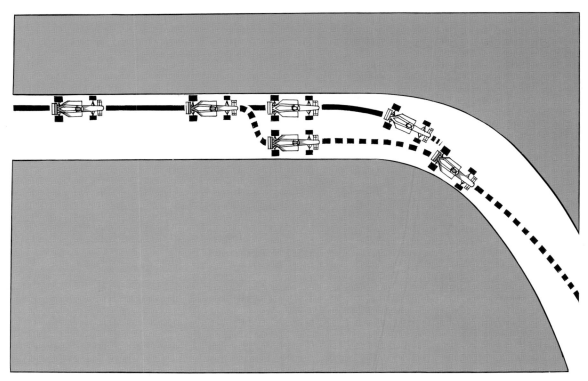

a mistake, even if it is only to drift slightly off line. These feints – which in the case of novices are instead failed attempts at overtaking when it is impossible to pass – have to be unexpected in order to convince the man in front. The planning of these strategies is fundamental to a successful overtaking move.

Here are some rules: never let an opponent know where you are faster than him (or where he is slower) so that you do not lose the element of surprise, allowing your rival to take defensive action. You must act decisively, without the slightest hesitation: once a decision has been taken, it has to be carried through. Don't fall into the rhythm of the driver you are chasing, but keep your own. Have the strength of purpose to run an independent race, in the firm belief that the 'study phase'

Overtaking can be made easier by slipstreaming if you are racing on a circuit with long straights. You have to catch your opponent and tail him. By staying within a distance of 60 metres from the rear of the car in front you will suffer less aerodynamic resistance and, given equal power, will have more speed. This is why, when approaching a corner, a driver can pull out of the slipstream and overtake his opponent thanks to the difference in speed.

will be short-lived. Use your intuition and imagination, because the one thing that is not legislated for in motor racing is overtaking.

In order to remind a novice driver of the fundamental rules, before a race the mechanics repeat phrases like 'determination, surprise, speed': they are effective. If you realise that you have been following your opponent too long, and that nothing has happened, you can drop back, find new motivation and attack again with more fervour: in the great majority of cases something positive will come out of it.

This is something that young drivers from the lower formulae in some countries where it has become common to give in to the car ought to try. If a driver starts from pole and gains three-tenths of a second on his opponents, that is almost certain to be his advantage at the end, as no one will have tried to challenge him for the lead. This happens not only among the leading group, but also halfway down the grid. If a car is lapping four-hundredths of a second faster than another, the slower driver will simply accept that he is lapping four-hundredths slower each lap. The logic is right, but this is not the right spirit with which to approach motor racing. In the past there were drivers who loved to fight and only wanted to win. They might not have been great technicians or test drivers, but they brought colour to the sport and excited the crowds.

The great majority of the overtaking that a top driver has to do in a Grand Prix involves drivers slower than himself. In this case we talk of lapping, because these drivers will lose a lap when they are passed. This operation, which should in theory be trouble free, as the drivers being lapped are supposed to give way, in fact involves a high degree of risk because, unlike overtaking, these moves are not planned. This can lead to misunderstandings which develop into incidents where the blame is usually levelled at the lapped driver, sometimes unfairly. Even a top driver can show indecision while lapping, and this can lead the man in front to misread his intentions, closing the door when the faster driver is already committed to overtaking.

One of the fundamental rules for a successful overtaking move is to avoid indecision, as this may lead to misunderstandings. So far we have seen what a driver has to do to overtake an opponent. But what if he is the one who is being shadowed by a rival? Then things are distinctly less fun. You could say that attack is the best form of defence, but if a car is put under pressure by another, there is not much attacking to be done; instead you have to defend, in the full meaning of the word.

The first weapons at our disposal are the rear-view mirrors. They must be looked at constantly: it is best not to do it haphazardly but to select points of reference and check them at every bend. In this way we will be able to tell if the gap to those following is increasing or decreasing.

As we have already seen, every driver, except for very rare exceptions, has weak spots. If we discover that the driver following has spotted our weakness (the way we take a bend, for example) and is getting closer every lap, the only option is to try and take it faster. At this stage it's best not to adopt a defensive line and stay in the middle of the bend, because this will only slow us down and allow the chaser to whittle away at the gap. Only when there are no other options do we choose the defensive line. If our opponent is faster, he will overtake us before long, so this manoeuvre is very useful at the beginning of a race, when the positions are not yet fixed

and overtaking is easier, and at the end, when we want our opponent to understand we do not intend to give an inch.

If, after sliding a bit in a bend, he slipstreams us on the next straight, the only thing we can do is to brake as late as possible, never more than a metre from the outside kerb on entry, discouraging any thought he might have of outbraking us. Weaving in the middle of the straight or switching to the inside just as he does so is not very effective, and is not correct anyway. Braking is the most important aspect of the defensive strategy when faced by a determined opponent. We cannot check our mirrors at this point, so we don't know where he is until we see him (or feel him) beside us. As we brake on the straight before turning into the corner there are three possibilities. The first is that he has given up and will try again on the next bend: in this case, realising that he is still in our slipstream or was only feinting, we can take the corner as if we were on our own.

If instead our rival has pulled out of the slipstream and is trying to pass us under braking, but our car is still ahead, we can close the door on him, taking the racing line we want: it is up to him to make sure he does not hit us. The last possibility is the worst one for us: when his attack under braking is successful and he is ahead (even if only by half a metre) at the entry to the bend. Then we have to relinquish our position, yet remain ready to take advantage if he misjudges his braking or is too fast going into the bend. The main point is this: never give up and never lose heart.

While Jean Alesi takes his line in his Ferrari, Ayrton Senna outbrakes Thierry Boutsen. To do this the Brazilian has had to move to the inside and delay his braking to the last moment. The picture was taken on the Phoenix street circuit.

CHAPTER 19

USING THE SLIPSTREAM

When racing on circuits where the average speed is very high, faster than 210 km/h, it becomes essential to know how to slipstream in order to overtake. The car preceding us, by cutting into the air ahead of us, creates a space behind it free from turbulence and wind resistance. In other words, if, to tackle a straight at 260 km/h, a car on its own has to exert 600 horsepower, another car slipstreaming the first will need only 570 bhp.

With equal power, therefore, the following car has another 30 bhp in reserve to increase its speed. Clearly, to slipstream another single-seater, the driver must be slightly faster than his quarry, just enough to catch him up. Once he starts to slipstream he will feel the car begin to accelerate. This does not happen very close to the car in front, but about 60 metres away.

This will allow him to get on the tail of his rival with a decent speed advantage, which will help him overtake. Of course you need to judge the moment to pull out of the slipstream. Doing it too early means not making full use of the opportunity to increase your speed, so that when you draw alongside the other car you will not be quite as fast as you could have been; making your move too late means you will be unable to overtake because the bend is too near and you have to start braking.

In the latter case you cannot make use of your speed and even risk losing contact with the car in front. And by getting too close to his gearbox, you enter an area of turbulence (immediately behind the car) which plays havoc with your own aerodynamics.

Experience is important for slipstreaming, as it is not so much a question of sensitivity as of exploiting to the full the factors involved.

It may not look like it, but slipstreaming is

a dangerous business. It can lead to an increase in the water and oil temperatures, because being so close to another car means that the flow of cool air to the radiators is restricted.

A less experienced driver may slipstream a rival for a number of laps and without noticing, so preoccupied is he with the heat of the battle, that his temperatures are rising, and he may break his engine. It is a wise move to drop back to about ten metres behind if you cannot overtake within a reasonable amount of time, in order to let the engine cool off and return to the right temperatures. This can also be of benefit to the driver, as you can then renew the attack with greater fervour.

Aerodynamic efficiency is reduced when you are slipstreaming. As there is less air to work with, our aerodynamic devices will create less load on the wheels: it's as if we had smaller wings. This can be dangerous in the big sweeping bends, where the tyres are under stress, yet are loaded less than before. In this case it is best to accept that you have less grip and proceed with caution – so no sudden movements or changes of direction.

Another thing to be aware of when slipstreaming is that when it is very hot you have less aerodynamic efficiency: if we find ourselves in a situation of this kind, the slipstream will be less powerful.

CHAPTER 20

PIT SIGNALS AND RACE TACTICS

When a driver sprints off the start line, he is not going into battle alone, but has the very valuable help of his team. In the Sixties, many of the Formula 1 drivers started their careers as mechanics: this helped them notice that something was going wrong and they could take the right course of action.

Nowadays there is a computer on board which transmits to the driver and to the pits all the data that dozens of sensors relay about the car's behaviour. There are sensors which monitor the engine and its functions, checking temperatures and maximum revs, and others which record variations in the tyre pressures.

The onboard computer will tell a driver how much fuel is left and how many laps he can maintain his current pace for: this was a very important aid in the turbo era as there was a finite amount of fuel allowed in each race.

The driver can gather data initially from his own cockpit, then he can call back to the pits via the radio with which all cars are fitted and speak to the race engineer. The radio can also be used for emergencies, such as a sudden puncture and thus an earlier pit stop than had been planned.

When this system was not in use, the driver had no choice but to appear suddenly in the pit lane and waste time explaining to the team what the matter was, or he might, if the problem wasn't so bad, give a hand-signal to the pits to warn them that he would be coming in on the next lap.

The radio can be used by the race engineer or team manager to warn the driver of a mechanical problem of which he may not be aware, or to bring forward a tyre change. Usually a team is loath to use the radio, because it might do so at the wrong moment and distract the driver.

Pit boards are still used in Formula 1 to

inform the drivers of the gaps to those in front and behind. Pit boards also give the number of laps completed (or how many there are to go) and the team's instructions regarding the positions held and pace of the race (for example 'slow' means 'hold your position'). Here we have already entered the area of race tactics. There are drivers who have successfully made tactics the key to their approach and exploited them to the full. A mature driver must have an understanding of race tactics, he cannot always follow his nose.

This is something that requires experience and the tempering of your aggression: a driver who sees the race like a chess game is easy to spot as he stops getting involved in accidents and aims for points and not just wins.

This kind of driving is very effective over a season when aiming for the world title. Choosing the best set-up (a less fast car, but one that will be reliable) or the right time to stop for tyres, and knowing when to relinquish a position when the race situation calls for it are all part of this.

The dialogue with the pits is very important for a driver who uses his head, and this is why, when choosing a team, you have to give careful consideration to its management.

CHAPTER 21
FLAG SIGNALS

A driver does not communicate only with the pits during a race. The circuit marshals are trained to give the drivers a continuous update on the dangers which may arise in the course of the race and the decisions that the circuit and race directors may take during the event.

The marshals use flags to communicate with the driver, who must be able to keep an eye on the trackside, where the marshals stand, while he is driving.

Most of the time the flags warn the driver of danger – if a car is about to lap him, or if there is oil on the track, a circuit vehicle which is proceeding at low speed, or a mechanical failure which he has failed to notice – so it is for reasons of safety that you have to pay attention to flags and marshals. And they can also have an important bearing on positions: if, for example, we are overtaken while the marshals are waving yellow flags (the symbol for danger instructing drivers to slow down), we may be able to have our adversary disqualified at the end of the race as he has broken the rules. The flag signals used at the circuits are shown on the opposite page.

National flag: used to give the start if there isn't a green light.

Danger on track, slow down, no overtaking.

Danger, service vehicle or ambulance on the track.

Give way, someone is trying to overtake.

Danger, oil on track.

End of danger zone, shown after the yellow flag.

Stop, race has been suspended, return to the pits immediately.

Dangerous driving; a warning is issued only once.

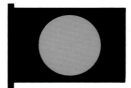

Mechanical problems, return to the pits.

Return to pits, disqualification, accompanied by driver's number.

The end of the race.

CHAPTER 22

FITNESS TRAINING

To get to the top in motor racing, to drive a Formula 1 car in one of the leading teams, you have to have certain qualities in the right proportion. One of them has always been much admired, and is now more important than ever: consistency. What matters is not a single outstanding move but your performance across the full duration of a race, a racing season, a year and indeed your career.

It is no use a driver performing at his best for the first four or five laps, then fading away, squandering a good position and considerable amounts of money, as well as the chance to confirm his place in that team. Clearly consistency is not simply a natural talent within a driver, but the outcome of a long and tough physical fitness programme which will allow us to give our best at all times and reach the end of a race – even the toughest – as fresh as we were at the start.

Now that the lateral force in a bend has been measured at 4G (but soon we will reach 5G, and there are some drivers who claim we already have), a driver cannot rely simply on a robust constitution and a basic fitness regime: he must instead work on very detailed programmes to combat the fatigue experienced during a Grand Prix race and protect the body against the stresses induced by sitting in an F1 car. The programme divides into two parts: the winter phase is the toughest and forms the basis for the racing season; the training you do during the season is aimed at maintaining the level you have achieved, and is less demanding in terms of time and energy.

Winter training might begin a month after the end of the season and extend to the start

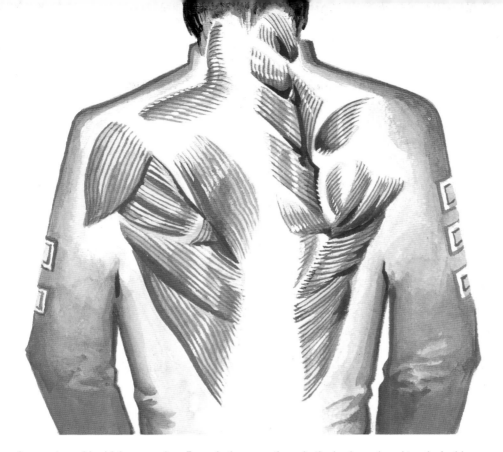

The muscles most used in driving a modern Formula 1 car are those in the back, neck and trunk. And because of the violent lateral and longitudinal forces, which can reach four times the value of gravity, that is 4G – and soon we will reach 5G – drivers must exercise these muscles.

of the next one. Nowadays the trend is to have a complete break until a couple of months before the first race. Most teams now have a test driver, so the race driver can cut back on the stressful pre-season testing: it really depends on the individual – it is a question of psychology – and the terms of his contract. I will not drive until just before the first race, and many other drivers prefer doing this, so as to start the season with a greater will to drive and increased aggression.

Most F1 drivers undertake winter training,

the period varying from one to two months. At Ferrari, who are among the leaders in fitness thinking, they take the drivers to train at altitude, to increase the level of red cells. Not all teams take it this far, but all require a proper fitness programme.

Let's see how to organise ourselves and which exercises to do in the period of intensive training – exercises which are designed to achieve the proper balance between muscle mass and aerobic fitness.

Starting at 8.30 in the morning, we do a five-kilometre run, which after a month will be increased to 15 km. You can run in the open air, but also on a treadmill – which can be set at an angle of four degrees, and increased to six after 30 days. Running is the foundation of fitness for a driver. Only by running slowly will you get your heart used to an increase of effort over a period of time. During a race the heart is constantly operating at more than 160–170 beats per minute. At

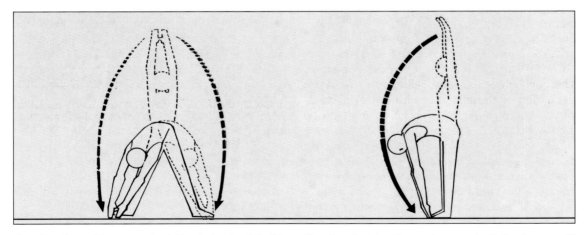

Standing, legs wide, arms raised. Touch the tip of the left foot with both hands, come back up and then touch the other foot. When bent over, you should stay down at least 20 seconds, lengthening muscles and tendons. Breathe in as you come up, breathe out going down.

Standing, feet together and arms raised. Bend over until you touch your toes. Stay in this position for at least 20 seconds, head tucked as low as possible. Breathe in coming up, breathe out on the way down.

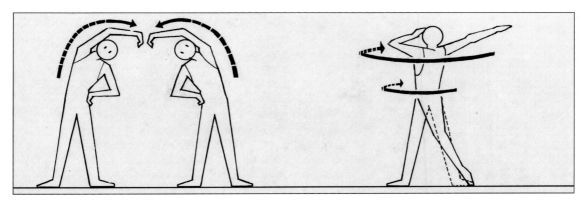

Bend the trunk to the right and then the left, keeping the back straight and not leaning forward. The arms have to follow the movement, which stops when we reach the bent position.

Twisting. Keeping the arms straight and raised to shoulder height, twist first to the right, then to the left. Note that the back must stay straight while the hips must rotate as little as possible.

times it reaches 200. As the maximum the heart can cope with is 220, it is easy to see how crucial it is to increase the heart's capacity.

By training we reach three objectives: we bring more oxygen to the muscles (and to the brain), rid the body of the excessive heat induced by exercise, and keep a constant, but reduced, circulation to other areas of the body (brain, intestine). There are also changes in the cardiovascular and respiratory areas: a reduction of the heartbeat and arterial pressure, an increase in the amount of blood pumped by each heart contraction, a lowering of the number of breaths taken, and an increase in lung capacity. Thus it is easy to see how running increases the body's resistance to external forces.

And here is an example for everyone: if, in the days of skirts and ground effect, the drivers had all been as fit as today's Grand Prix field, a great many unexplained accidents would not have happened because, for example, the supply of blood to the brain would always have been adequate. With the skirted

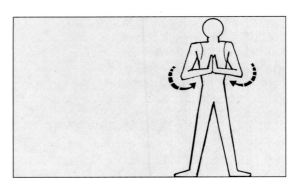

Standing, with feet shoulder-width apart. Join the palms of the hand behind your back, keeping it as straight as possible. If you can't join your palms, try and get them as close as possible.

cars, in some instances the brain was left for fractions of a second without oxygenated blood.

The immediate goal of running is to lower the heartbeat at rest.

The speed at which we can recuperate is another indication of our level of fitness and of the heart's condition. After two minutes' rest at the end of a 15 km run, the pulse of an F1 driver is around 80–85. To get the best results, the running must be slow and the pulse must not go higher than 120. This is a fundamental point if running is to be part of a fitness programme.

Then we look at increasing muscle resistance. We only work on the areas affected by driving, and we don't consider increasing the power or bulk (which would lead to an increase in weight) but concentrate on muscle stamina as the muscles have to last the length of a tough Grand Prix race. An increase in muscle bulk would also put pressure on the heart, as it would have to pump more blood into larger muscles, thus leaving less blood for other parts of the body. Thus we have to do many sets of repetitions with light weights: starting with a series of ten repeated three times with only half a kilo of weight in each hand, and ending with a series of ten repeated eight times with two kilos per hand. We should spend an hour a day in the gym, starting with the top muscles and working down to allow an even body development: first with the neck, then the arms, the upper body and finally the legs.

The neck requires particular attention, because it is subject to unusual stresses. The extraordinary grip of an F1 car, allied to the

Standing, feet shoulder-width apart, clasp hands at shoulder blade height, the left arm above the shoulder, the right arm below. Force progressively, first upwards, then downwards.

Sitting, legs crossed, lengthen the muscles in the forearms by pushing with the opposite arm. Keep a degree of effort for at least 20 seconds.

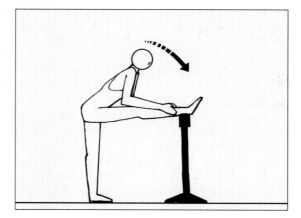

Raise the leg to hip height and lean it on a support. Grasp the calf and stretch by bending the upper body towards the foot. Once this is achieved, hold the position for at least 20 seconds.

Lying down, raise your legs until they are behind your head and touching the floor. Keeping your balance with your arms, straighten your legs as much as possible, and if this comes easily try straightening your upper body.

Sitting down, legs extended in front, fold one leg and bring it back behind you. To extend the quad muscles you must now bend the upper body behind you and support it with your legs. Hold for 20 seconds.

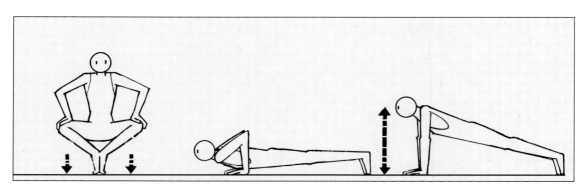

Sitting, back straight (very important this), bring your feet together and close to the groin. Then you must push down on the knees towards the floor.

When the stretching is over, it's a good idea to do two series of push-ups. The only proviso when doing this exercise, which everyone is familiar with, is to keep the back straight. Touch the floor with the chest, but don't stay down too long.

After push-ups, in order to stretch the muscles of the arms, torso and legs, this is a useful exercise. Do it in one motion and very slowly, always stretching at the start and the end.

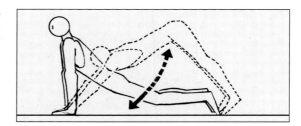

way bends have been built in recent years, has caused lateral acceleration factors to increase dramatically. A normally muscled person could not withstand these loads: this is why so many drivers seem to be bull necked, just like boxers.

Firstly the neck is subjected to resistance from the front, the sides and the back, but only using an arm. The pressure applied by the arm must not exceed six to eight seconds, the length of time it takes to go through a bend. After about four days, this exercise must be done with a helmet, which increases the total weight of the head by a kilo and a half. After eight days of training, we should increase the resistance by pushing against a rubber band. In all cases we should not force the neck for more than eight seconds.

From the neck we move to the arms. The exercises are not complicated and do not require special equipment. We just need two dumbells fitted with weights which will never exceed two kilos: this has nothing to do with body building. Here it is important to work slowly and using wide movements: it is not the number of repetitions that matters but how long we exercise for. After each set of exercises we must rest for as long as we exercised. This recuperation time must be strictly adhered to in order to avoid overtiring the muscles, which would affect performance. The muscles we must work on are the deltoids, the chest muscles, the forearms and the biceps. The upper body exercises come next and then those for the legs.

The abdominal and back muscles are essential to withstanding tiredness, because they support the work of the arms, which must rest on a solid foundation, and help prevent the sort of injuries which the stresses of driving an F1 car, with its very hard suspension, can lead to. You exercise the stomach

Rest your hand on the side of your head and push: the neck muscles react and try to keep the head upright. First with your right hand, then with the left.

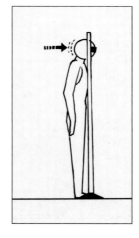

Lean your head against a rubber band and push against it. Then lean the side of the head and repeat the movement.

Lie on a bench and move your head up and down. The movements must be slow and continuous, with no sudden movements or stopping. The level of fitness is indicated by the number of repetitions you manage.

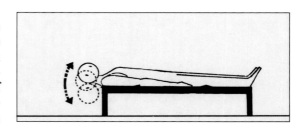

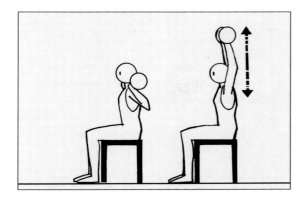

Sitting, clutching two weights of two kilos each held behind your head, lift the weights until the arms are straight. The movements are slow and continuous and the back must be straight at all times.

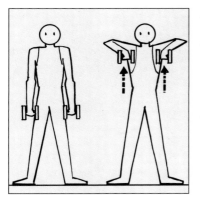

A weight in each hand, palms facing outwards, feet shoulder-width apart, lift the weights to the chest. Keep your back straight.

With arms at shoulder height and not fully stretched, rotate clockwise and then anti-clockwise. The exercise must be done with two-kilo weights in each hand.

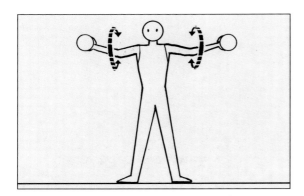

muscles by lying flat on your back and raising the upper body through 90 degrees. Your legs must be held by your fitness coach or tucked under some retaining object. The back is exercised by lying face down, with the ankles held as before, and lifting the upper body as far as possible. Ferrari have a rather energy-consuming method of exercising the legs: swimming with two 2-kilo lead weights strapped to the ankles. The drivers have to swim ten lengths of a 25-metre pool, stopping each time for as long as it has taken them to swim. If the pool is smaller than 25 metres, as often happens in mountain hotels, we will have to swim more lengths to equal the distance. And if there isn't a pool available, there is a valid alternative: leg bends.

At the end of the morning, having run and exercised the muscles, it is wise to have a bath to relax the tired muscles. In the afternoon we continue, this time working on stamina. If we are in the mountains, the best exercise is cross-country skiing: initially you will have to do at least five kilometres, and then progress to 15 km. The rest of the afternoon is for resting, so as to benefit from the exercises and avoid the trap of overtraining. In order to keep up our sporting aggression, twice a week we can play a game of tennis instead of cross-country skiing. But do beware of strains and pulls, which are always there ready to pounce.

Maintaining your fitness starts from the very first run, and some never let up the level of exercise, just adapting it to the racing and testing schedule. In other words, some drivers train just as hard in the season as they do through the winter. It depends on your prefer-

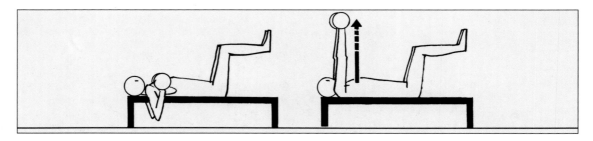

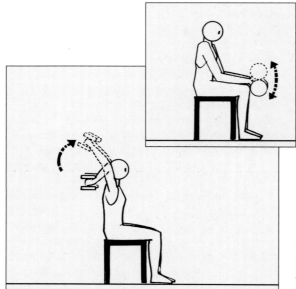

Lie on a bench and lift your legs to a 90-degree angle to avoid straining the lower back. Push up with the arms from the level of your chest. It is the chest muscles you are working on, and the movement must be slow and continuous.

To exercise the forearms, lift weights not exceeding two kilos. Sitting and with the forearms leaning on the knees, first do it with palms facing upwards, then downwards.

This is for the triceps. The arms must be folded behind the head and hold a two-kilo weight. Keep your elbows as close to your head as possible and raise your hand without straightening your arms completely.

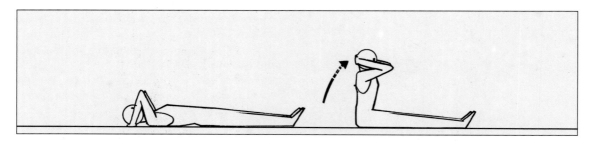

Sit-ups are done lying down and lifting the upper body until it is at 90 degrees to the legs. The back must be straight and the ankles must be held fast.

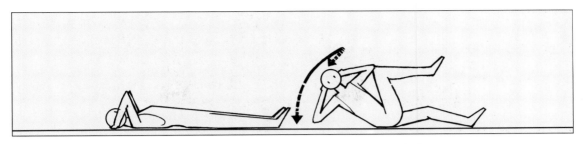

With hands behind your head, lift the upper body towards the right lifting the right leg and touching it with the left elbow. Then repeat on the opposite side.

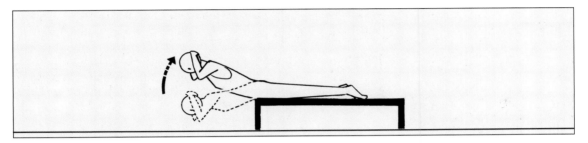

With the ankles held fast and facing downwards, do trunk raises. Avoid arching the back excessively on the up movement. A continuous movement will strengthen the back muscles.

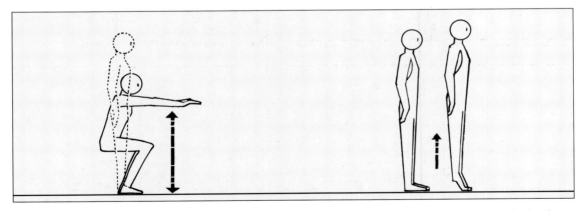

To strengthen the legs, the best exercise is still the knee bend. Feet together and back straight, bend your legs until the thighs are parallel to the floor. The arms should be held out in front.

Feet together, back straight, we lift off our heels, always keeping as straight as possible. This is for the calf muscles. It is also useful for balance, if done with the eyes closed.

ence, whether you need to improve your levels of stamina, and the system favoured by your coach.

Most choose to ease off and just maintain the levels reached in winter. Thus we should run twice weekly, slowly and for 15–20 km, and also have two sessions with weights. It is best to do these exercises on alternate days, in order to give the body a chance to recuperate. Those drivers who hate running can find equivalent exercises. You can choose between a six- to eight-kilometre walk on soft ground (grass) – which must not be level – or a round of golf (a very popular sport among F1 drivers), which usually covers the same amount and type of ground as the walk.

Those who want to do something more strenuous and still not run can swim, continuously doing 20 lengths of a 25-metre pool, the equivalent of 500 metres. On race weekends, a driver can walk twice the length of the circuit, the second time maybe at a slow run, keeping his pulse to 120. This is doubly useful. Firstly it will get the body used to the kinds of stresses it will experience over the weekend, and secondly it will remind the driver of a circuit he may not have seen for a year. After going round the track, you should stretch for at least 15 minutes. On the Thursday, or Wednesday, you should also do a few repetitions with weights.

As we spend so much time in hotel rooms, many drivers use weights that can be filled with water and are therefore very easy to pack away. The weight can also be increased or decreased with ease. Stretching is always very important, especially if you do not have a masseur.

When doing these exercises, which are not difficult, you should hold the position for at least 20 seconds. This does not apply to all exercises (some have to be done without stopping), but it is important to do it when necessary because this way the muscle is gently stretched and relaxed.

Driving is essentially a matter of control, where the man does not create the movement. The right fitness programme allows us to go about our business in the best way possible and at the highest levels for the length of the race. So stamina, perseverance and a clear mind are directly related to the level of fitness of the driver.

CHAPTER 23

DIET

T o achieve and maintain top physical and mental condition, it is essential to follow the right diet in order to nourish the body. There is an analogy with a Formula 1 car, which needs good high-octane fuel.

Let's see how a driver's diet should be planned. Breakfast must be abundant and nourishing, to provide sufficient energy to reach midday in the right metabolic condition. The English (who are well represented in the world of Formula 1) have long had this habit, which the Italians and French, for example, do not have. Rather than their customary coffee and croissant, you should have a nice cup of tea sweetened with fructose.

The reason for using fructose is that it is a pure sugar (so it has the same sweetening effect as sugar) which is less of a burden for the liver. It is easy to find and it is usually sold in sachets. The right diet calls for at least two slices of dried bread or two slices of wholemeal, jam or honey, and a boiled egg, cooked for three minutes (the right time to guarantee digestibility) with a little salt, two slices of Parma ham or 50 grammes of Parmesan cheese. At the end (and this applies to every meal) you should drink a glass of water with some lemon juice, which should be kept in the mouth before swallowing. A glass of water and lemon contributes to the right intestinal pH balance, and this is why it should be taken at the end of every meal.

The right vitamin intake should include vitamins A, C and E, together with the mineral selenium. Vitamin C is sold in powder form and you should take a gramme a day; the

This is what a Formula 1 champion like Ayrton Senna has for breakfast: fresh fruit, wholemeal toast with a thin spread of butter and jam, honey and tea. Diet is fundamental to the preparation and conditioning of drivers. Alcohol and big meals are banned from the table, and in their place are easily digestible foods.

other vitamins and selenium are easily available in pill form. You should take one a day. Vitamins have an antioxidant function, lessen the effects of tiredness and fight the deterioration of the cells. They are not energy giving (carbohydrates) or body building (proteins): their function is more a protective one.

At lunchtime and in the evening it is important to get used to a single-component dish, that is food all of the same type. The Mediterranean diet, the most balanced of all, nevertheless does not provide a clear nutritional structure. The single-type diet instead allows us to separate the different foods, even before our digestive system does, and this is of help in digesting our meals. Foods are divided into three main groups: carbohydrates (or sugars), fats and proteins. Carbohydrates are purely energy-giving, and provide the main source of energy for endurance sports, such as Formula 1.

The reserves our body stores are relatively limited and will be exhausted after about one hour of activity. It is therefore important to top up your carbohydrate level constantly in order to have further energy reserves always available.

Fats are stored under the skin and it is this source of energy that we turn to when carbohydrates have run out. This will happen after about an hour or an hour and a half, but if a driver is topping up properly with carbohydrates he should never have to rely on fat. If you want to lose weight, you have to extend your training beyond the one and a half hour point (every minute is effective after this time) and cut down the daily intake of carbohydrates. Fat should never be taken before a race or any sporting event, because twice as much oxygen is required for it to be assimilated as for carbohydrates. The quantity one must consume daily is minimal.

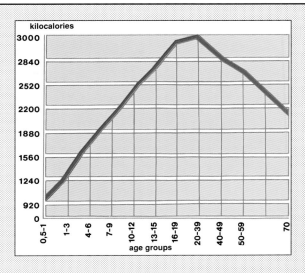

kilocalories

age groups

The graph shows how daily energy requirements reach their peak between the ages of 20 and 39.

CALORIES OF VARIOUS FOODS AND DRINKS

MEAT	Calories						
Lamb	270	Mozzarella	280	Tuna in oil	245	Dried figs	380
Beef	100	Parmesan	360				
Liver	130	Gouda	350	**MILK**		**VEGETABLES**	
Pork (lean)	160			Ordinary	70	Asparagus	24
Pork (fat)	350	**BREAD and PASTA**		Skimmed	40	Aubergines	32
Cooked ham	285	White bread	255	Condensed	320	Spinach	25
Raw ham	330	Pasta	350			Courgettes	47
Fat ham	430	Egg pasta	380	**FRUIT**		Carrots	42
Salami	350	Bread sticks	420	Oranges	45	Artichokes	70
Chicken	220	Dry biscuits	415	Bananas	95	Fresh string beans	35
Turkey	280			Mandarins	42	Fresh beans	180
Veal	150	**EGGS**		Apricots	40	Cucumber	15
		Soft boiled	75	Cherries	50	Lettuce	20
FATS		Yolk	60	Grapefruit	40	Peas	80
Butter	750			Pears	40	Peppers	15
Margarine	740	**FISH**		Peaches	50	Tomatoes	19
Olive oil	920	Perch	100	Medlars	60	Potatoes	80
Vegetable oil	880	Trout	90	Figs	75	Onions	40
		Fresh mackerel	60	Strawberries	35		
		Salted mackerel	110	Plums	55	**ALCOHOL**	
CHEESES		Sole	75	Apples	45	Wine	75-95
Low fat	190	Mullet	80	Grapes	85	Fortified wines	100-160
Bel Paese	310	Grey mullet	70	Walnuts	490	Shot of brandy	90-200
Emmenthal	395	Pilchard	80	Chestnuts	190	Aperitif	90-140

These figures are for 100 grammes of raw food. The calories in drinks are given per centilitre

Proteins, which are less important from an energy point of view, are necessary for an organism to build particular body structures, such as muscles. The daily protein intake is equivalent to a gramme for every body weight kilo. Thus the ideal single-type diet for a driver involves a midday meal based on carbohydrates like pasta, rice, potatoes, corn and pulses (peas, lentils, beans, soya, chickpeas and similar). For supper, the meal should be based on proteins (meat, cheese, fish and milk).

When at the circuit for a test session or a race (from Friday to Sunday), when the body is subjected to heavy stress, it is a good idea to have an early lunch at 11 a.m. based on carbohydrates like pasta or rice, with oil and Parmesan cheese (rich in mineral salts). Breakfast stays as normal, while at 12.30 you should eat fruit, and at three o'clock plenty of cake. In the evening, especially before a race, you should eat white and lean meat (chicken or rabbit) or fish, and of course vegetables as a side dish. If you can't eat pasta or rice, which is hard to come by in the Formula 1 paddock, you can make do with a banana, three wholemeal biscuits and some cereal bars, or the usual banana with a toasted sandwich and salad, tomato, mozzarella cheese and two slices of ham.

An important aspect of a driver's dietary balance is the liquid intake. During heavy training sessions, or in a race, the body sweats and loses a lot of liquid. You can lose up to 1.5–2 litres of fluid in an hour: when running you can lose up to 3 litres. Sixty to seventy per cent of our body weight is made up by water; a loss of 4 per cent causes a 40 per cent drop in the body's effectiveness, and when the figure rises to 10 per cent the loss of liquids may lead to serious disorders. A loss of water also means a reduction in the level of

The Ideal Menu for a Racing Driver

LUNCH

A piece of wholemeal
bread or white bread

Vegetables dressed with
balsamic vinegar, a
quarter of a lemon
(squeezed), two spoonfuls
of extra-virgin olive oil
with 0.6 of acidity, sea
salt

Long pasta (spaghetti, tagliatelle) in a sauce of tomato, basil (or parsley or rocket or spring onions), extra-virgin olive oil (or 100 per cent vegetable margarine), a spoonful of Parmesan cheese (but only in winter)

Short pasta (rigatoni, penne) . . .

. . . in a sauce of 100 per cent vegetable margarine, a sachet of saffron, or a spoonful of mayonnaise

. . . or in a sauce of extra-virgin olive oil, with the addition of egg yolk, ten grammes of margarine, and a spoonful of cottage cheese

. . . or in a sauce of extra-virgin olive oil, a sachet of saffron, San Daniele ham chopped and sautéd in a pan without oil

Fruit: half a melon or a slice of water melon or a quarter of pineapple or two kiwis

Lemon sorbet or ice cream

The table gives an indication of the choices available for
a racing driver's midday meal. It is an appetising menu.

mineral salts (especially sodium, potassium, chlorine and magnesium) present in the body. Water loss must be made up with an intake of at least 2–3 litres on the same day. Mineral salts can be replenished either through food (such as fresh vegetables or dried fruit) or in the form of specially prepared drinks (especially magnesium and potassium).

Liquid intake, to replenish loss of water and mineral salts, is strongly recommended. Tiredness, like extreme cold, numbs sensations of thirst and hunger, and this can lead to a dangerous underestimation of the importance of calories. At the end of a particularly tough exertion, if there isn't a specialised drink at hand, you should take one or two spoonfuls of salt in water: it tastes awful, but is extremely beneficial. When the physical effort is not so big, salt and water replenishment can come from eating vegetables and a glass of water with lemon at the end of a meal. Some drivers never drink when eating, in order to maintain the right level of water and mineral salts.

There should always be a perfect balance of the substances that form our body, but at times there are alterations or losses. This is why it is important to have regular check-ups (at least three times a year). It is particularly important to monitor the level of iron in the body, as you lose a lot through sweating. The remedy, if needed, must be under medical supervision and based on iron products.

The Ideal Menu for a Racing Driver

DINNER

Crudité (dressed with extra-virgin olive oil, sea salt): carrots, celery, tomatoes, radishes, heart of artichoke and wholemeal bread (or white) and potato purée

chicken breast, asparagus (or spinach), sautéd in lemon and a little oil

. . . or skinless chicken legs, wrapped in ham, three oven-baked potatoes

. . . or 250–300 grammes of grilled fish (sole, swordfish or similar), oven-baked spinach and a scrambled egg; lemon sorbet

. . . or fillet of veal wrapped in raw ham, grilled courgettes and aubergines; two kiwis (or a quarter of a pineapple)

. . . or potato purée with margarine (no butter, no milk), two poached eggs covered with ham; ice cream

. . . or beef carpaccio (or chicken breast or ham), dressed with rocket, raw mushrooms, celery, carrots, two olives, two slices of Parmesan (only in winter, though), extra-virgin olive oil, balsamic vinegar, a quarter of a lemon, squeezed, sea salt; a meringue

There are many choices for dinner as well. All meals must be accompanied by non-alcoholic drinks.

CHAPTER 24

PSYCHOLOGY

In addition to physical training, some drivers also devote time to psychological preparation, in order to remain lucid, calm and objective inside and outside the cockpit. Maybe in ten years' time this kind of training will be as crucial as the physical kind to reaching the top in Formula 1. It is a fascinating new approach which is in its infancy. Let's take a closer look at it.

Broadly speaking any kind of mental training which aims to increase a driver's effectiveness at the wheel of a racing car must start from the assumption that victory is a consequence of the work done. With this attitude, victory ceases to be the main objective and is replaced by the quest for perfection in the various factors which contribute to victory, such as fitness training, setting up the car, managing a set of tyres properly, knowledge of the race tracks and so on, always focusing on smaller and smaller things. Thus when a driver takes to the track during timed qualifying, he will not have uppermost in his mind the idea of setting the fastest lap. Instead he will try to produce a perfect lap, overcoming the difficulties of the track, optimising his own performance and concentrating on all those details which make a decisive difference.

Looked at in this way, pole position (or victory) is the consequence of the work done in different areas. The driver must not succumb to the pressures of winning, of qualifying, of the team members around him or the sponsors, who expect a result. For a driver, getting into the car must be like going to the office for a top manager: it is his everyday job. In order to become accustomed to remaining unemo-